THIS COPY OF
MASSEY FERGUSON
35 & 65 MODELS
In Detail
IS SIGNED BY THE AUTHOR

Mike Thorne

MICHAEL THORNE

MASSEY FERGUSON
35 & 65 Models

In Detail

MASSEY FERGUSON
35 & 65 Models

In Detail

BY MICHAEL THORNE

Herridge & Sons

Published in 2014 by
Herridge & Sons Ltd
Lower Forda, Shebbear
Beaworthy, Devon EX21 5SY

© Copyright Michael Thorne 2014

Designed by Ray Leaning, MUSE Fine Art & Design Ltd
Special photography by Andrew Morland

ISBN 978-1-906133-53-5
Printed in China

Dedication

This book is dedicated to the memory of Harold Beer, family man,
farmer and Ferguson enthusiast – a truly gentle man.

Author's Acknowledgments

Thanks must go to Herridge and Sons for asking me to write this
book. Like my *Ferguson TE20 In Detail*, this was a scary commitment
but a joy to produce, not only from the creative act of writing but
also the communication with fellow Massey Ferguson enthusiasts
who are always generous in sharing their knowledge and time: that
has been a great source of encouragement.

I should make it clear that Chapter One is the work of David Lory
and Bob Sybrandy based in America. This valuable contact was established by Julie Browning and Peter Smith. To all four I am most grateful
for providing fresh insights into the Eastern Hemisphere tractors.

I am indebted to Alan Starley, who agreed to read the whole
draft. His comments are worked into the text where appropriate.
Further positive comments and suggestions were made by Ernie
Luxton and George French. Both have had a lifetime of experience in
the agricultural machinery field.

Jeremy Burgess, one-time licensee director at AGCO, suggested
useful enhancements and also helped me make several new contacts.
He also kindly offered to write the Foreword.
My thanks also to John Farnworth and Bob Dickman for material that
appears in Chapter Eight – Overseas.

My late friend Harold Beer shared with me his knowledge and his
comprehensive library of Massey Ferguson material. I am also grateful
to Chris Messingham of Friends of Ferguson Heritage for providing
data that appears in the appendix.

My thanks must also go to Gail McKechnie for continuously
working from my handwritten drafts and dealing with correspondence
over the internet.

I was very glad that Herridge & Sons chose Andrew Morland to
carry out the commissioned photography, a most positive contribution
to this work.

Finally, thanks to Alison Harding for support and encouragement
throughout this project.

Contents

Foreword by Jeremy Burgess   6

Introduction – Massey Harris and Harry Ferguson   8

Chapter 1: The Beginnings – TO20, TO35, TO40   15

Chapter 2: The FE35   32

Chapter 3: The MF35   48

Chapter 4: The MF65   62

Chapter 5: Implements   78

Chapter 6: Accessories and Conversions   110

Chapter 7: Overseas   120

Chapter 8: MF35 and 65 in Use Today   130

Appendix A: Serial numbers, FE35, MF35, MF65   132
Appendix B: Prefix letters, MF35 and 65   132
Appendix C: First build dates, FE35 and MF35   133
Appendix D: Build dates, MF65   134
Appendix E: Last build dates, FE35, MF35, MF65   134
Appendix F: Comparison, MF35X and competitors   135

Foreword

I first met Mike Thorne some years ago when I was handling the movement of the Massey Ferguson Heritage Collection from its base in Banner Lane, Coventry, following the closure of the factory. Mike kindly agreed to provide a long-term home for some of our machines, and they remain on display today in the magnificent Coldridge Collection. Subsequently I was able to secure some other items from the factory for Mike's collection before the demolition team moved in, including the doors to the Banner Lane "Ferguson Centre". So began a firm friendship and I soon came to appreciate the depth of knowledge and passion Mike has for all things Ferguson and Massey Ferguson.

The history of the agricultural tractor has been one of steady evolution over more than 100 years, and several machines have been particularly important in their contribution to the story. The introduction of the Ferguson 35 in 1956 was arguably one of the most significant milestones in tractor history. Its evolution into the MF35, particularly with the fitment of the three-cylinder Perkins engine in 1959, was to lead to what has become an iconic tractor design.

Harry Ferguson's vision of facilitating affordable mechanisation for farmers the world over was realised with the famous Ferguson TE20 and the comprehensive range of matching implements and accessories. The 35 and 65 tractors took that vision a step further,

with higher outputs and levels of performance never seen before. By the end of production these famous tractors were to be found at work in over 150 countries around the globe, and even to this day they are sought after on the used market, exported from Europe, repaired and rebuilt to embark on a second and often very arduous life in a developing nation in Africa, the Far East or South America. Their performance, reliability and ease of repair and maintenance have ensured their enduring popularity, and they are a true testament to the design and manufacturing teams in the USA and in Coventry who created and enhanced these machines throughout their production life.

Through the very active Massey Ferguson Licensee division the MF35 and 65 tractors were dispatched in kit form from Coventry for assembly in a number of major markets. Gradual developments led to the point where the whole tractor could be produced locally, and today, more than 50 years later, tractors of the same basic design, or very close derivatives, remain in production in several countries. My career at Massey Ferguson covered numerous jobs, initially as design engineer, then Tractor Quality Manager at the Coventry plant, and later I gained first-hand knowledge of the licensing process and its legacy during several years heading up the Licensee Operations. It is fair to say that probably no other tractor design in history

An MF35X from the Coldridge Collection: the ultimate development of the range.

has contributed more to feeding the world's population than the MF35 and its direct descendants.

In this new book Mike Thorne has chronicled the story behind the 35 and 65 tractors, their key features and variants, in a way not achieved before. Painstakingly researched and using machines in Mike's Coldridge Collection as reference points, the book contains much new material and many previously unpublished photographs. An essential work for tractor enthusiasts young and old, it confirms the significance of these classic machines to the agricultural industry.

Jeremy Burgess
Former Director Licensee Operations
Massey Ferguson

Introduction

Massey-Harris and Harry Ferguson

Few machines can claim as much positive impact on the lives of so many as the Massey Ferguson 35 tractor and its variants. Thanks to worldwide distribution and innovations in mechanisation, the MF35's benefits to farming cannot be underestimated. Today, with the same basic design still in production and millions of machines working hard around the globe, it remains as relevant to feeding the world's population as it did during its development in the 1950s.

Growing from the 1953 merger of two great tractor manufacturers, the MF35 combined the creative efforts and hugely popular products of Massey-Harris and Ferguson to become the first in a legendary line of Massey Ferguson-badged tractors. It took all that was great about the TO35 and Ferguson FE35 (and, of course, Ferguson's revolutionary TE20) and improved farm production internationally - from the UK, Europe and America to emerging agricultural economies in the Middle East, Asia and Africa.

Later joined by the scaled-up MF65 and an increasingly useful list of implements and accessories, Massey Ferguson's clever, cost-effective and user-friendly machines truly made farming available to all.

Before we launch into the story of the 35 and 65 tractors that are the subject of this book, we will consider briefly the backgrounds of Massey and of Harris, and of their development until their eventual merger with Ferguson. Then we will consider the evolution of Harry Ferguson

until the merger with Massey-Harris that was announced to the public on 17 August 1953, thus creating Massey-Harris-Ferguson. By the autumn of 1957 this name was shortened to Massey Ferguson, as it is known today under the ownership of AGCO (Allis-Gleaner Corporation).

Massey-Harris

The Massey family descended from a line of hard-working, God-fearing Methodists who left Cheshire in about 1630 to escape the oppression of the established Church of England, facing challenges and finding freedom in North America and Canada. Daniel Massey was a pioneering farmer who cleared pine forest to the north of Lake Ontario to create his holding. His son, also Daniel, was born in 1798 and went on to set up the firm of Massey, which made and traded in basic farm tools and simple implements. Daniel Jnr's business prospered and he retired in 1855, but in the following year he died aged 58. His son, Hart Almerrin Massey, who had worked in the firm, formally took over its running.

There are strong parallels in the development of the Harris side of the company, which was also formed by descendants of Protestants who left England for America in the seventeenth century and moved north to Canada in the early nineteenth. The founder of the Harris firm of farm implement manufacturers was Alanson Harris, who started his business by purchasing a most modest foundry in 1857

Opposite page: Massey-Harris advertised for many years on the back cover of the Christmas edition of the Toronto Globe *supplement. Here they are emphasising their exports worldwide in 1901.*

and, like Massey, Harris's firm was progressive in the development of simple farm machines and prudent in the purchase of rival manufacturers when opportunities arose, thus not only knocking out some of the competition but also expanding the range of equipment it could offer to farmers.

For implement manufacturers in Canada, 1883 proved to be a bonanza year. By this time the self-tying binder had been developed into a reliable piece of harvesting machinery at an affordable price (about $300). The self-tying binder represented a major labour-saving breakthrough but competition was fierce, prompting the major producers to invest in colourful advertising. Meanwhile, a range of social facilities was established in order to maintain workers' loyalty.

For the 1890 harvest the French ministry of agriculture organised a four-day contest of binders from a selection of manufacturers. Massey proved victorious with its Toronto device. But Harris had been developing the open-end binder, which for the first time allowed straw of any length to be cut; this of course was a great benefit to the farmers of Europe.

By early 1891 Hart Massey felt it was time to relinquish the competition with Harris and to replace it with an amalgamation. By this point the two firms shared half of the farm machinery market in Canada. Hart Massey headed the merger's final discussions, with general manager Lyman Melvyn Jones representing Harris.

On 6 May 1891 a press release made the merger public, and thus the company Massey-Harris was born. Needless to say, the news sent shockwaves throughout the farm machinery sector and led to a storm of protest from farmers claiming it would reduce competition. In December 1891 came a further announcement: Massey-Harris had taken control of Patterson and Wisner, a producer of fine-quality farm implements. More protests followed, which Massey-Harris countered by reducing its prices.

In 1892 Massey-Harris gained a foothold in the Verity Plow Company. In 1895 the Bain Company, which produced farm carts and sleighs, became linked to Massey-Harris, thus broadening its sales base. In February 1896 Hart Massey died; his two sons, Walter and Chester, followed in the firm. Massey-Harris purchased Deyo-Macey (manufacturers of stationary petrol

engines used to drive barn machinery) in 1910, a year during which the firm also bought into Johnson Harvesting of New York. By 1928 Massey-Harris had purchased the J I Case Plow Works of Wisconsin, a deal that included the Wallis Farm tractor, a well-designed machine. It should be mentioned that a big part of Massey-Harris's success lay in the fact that over the years it had gradually built up a worldwide market by establishing dealerships in all developing countries, as well as manufacturing facilities far and wide.

The depression years of the early 1930s had far-reaching implications; so much that by 1934 Massey-Harris operations in America were experiencing severe losses of capital. Early in the winter of 1935 James S Duncan became general sales manager, 25 years after joining Massey-Harris. Soon afterwards, then-president T A Russell asked Duncan to make a full survey of Massey-Harris operations worldwide. Once completed, he was able to convince the firm's directors that losses could be limited to $250,000. At this point the general manager Bertram Burtswell resigned after a head-on confrontation with Duncan, whose plan had the board's backing; Duncan then succeeded Burtswell as general manager.

Around this time, a Massey-Harris engineer named Tom Carol had found an Italian firm operating in Argentina, which had developed what was termed a self-propelled reaper/thresher (a combine harvester in today's parlance). Duncan prudently asked his engineer to develop the concept in secret at the company's Toronto works, a decision that would provide long-term benefits for Massey-Harris.

The onset of World War II in Europe changed Massey-Harris's prospects for the better, because – like most manufacturing plants – its factories were switched to high levels of armament production. This meant most engineering establishments expanded and diversified rapidly in Britain, American and Canada. So, in a way, World War II probably saved Massey-Harris.

By 1944 Duncan was made president, heading a team of executives who were tough, knowledgeable men of determination and drive. The result was that, in April 1946, Massey-Harris was able to pay its first dividend in six years. The company had made a massive contribution to the war effort and had supplied the English war agricultural executive with farm machinery, notably its most successful MH21 self-propelled combine harvester. The design became something of a trailblazer, for with the backing of the American and Canadian governments 500 of these machines set to work in the harvest of 1944, starting in Texas in late June and heading northwards into Canada's wheat lands by September. They were known as the harvest brigade and by the end of the operation had jointly harvested one-and-a-half million acres of cereals. That year Massey-Harris produced 1800 combine harvesters.

During the latter part of World War II a group of astute businessmen built up the famous Argus Corporation, an investment firm. Over time they gained a measure of influence in several major companies, including Massey-Harris, and by 1948 had gained the control they were seeking. James S Duncan was still president, albeit a rather uncomfortable one, since the Argus group was, in reality, running the show. A number of the Argus men – Edward P Taylor, Eric Phillips, Wallace Cutren and Bud McDougald - were later involved in negotiations with Harry Ferguson that eventually led to the merger of Massey-Harris and Harry Ferguson Incorporated, a move that allowed two struggling companies to become one of the world's most famous names in farming.

Harry Ferguson

How did Harry Ferguson evolve from being the child of a hard-working, God-fearing farming couple to become the progenitor of the Ferguson System? It is not an exaggeration to say the Ferguson System of draft control (the use of the draft forces of the plough to increase the adhesion of the driving wheels of the tractor), was a revolution in mechanised farming; this system, albeit modified and developed, can be found integrated into the hydraulic systems of most tractors produced today.

Harry Ferguson was born on 4 November 1884, the fourth child of 11, to James and Mary Ferguson of Lake House Farm, Growell village, about 16 miles south of Belfast. The Ferguson side of the family had left Scotland during the seventeenth century.

Harry, at an early age, showed himself to be a bright and inquisitive child with an aptitude for mechanical things; he did not respond well to the drudgery of farming in those times, nor did he respond well to the devout religious upbringing that his parents thrust upon him. By

The Titan 10-20 was typical of the tractors of its period. It was made by International Harvester of Chicago between 1916 and 1922 and over 78,000 units were produced, of which more than 3000 were exported to the UK to boost food production during World War I. The model designation 10-20 related to drawbar horsepower and belt horsepower respectively.

his late teens he had developed his own agnostic beliefs that remained with him throughout his life. As the time approached for him to leave school at 14 he had seriously considered the possibility of emigrating to America or Canada, a common choice for many Irish youngsters. Who knows, had this happened he may have met up with the Massey-Harris organisation much earlier in his life.

But this was not to be the case. His eldest brother Joe, who had set up a car and motor-cycle repair garage in Belfast, suggested Harry could work for his developing firm. Harry was taken on as an apprentice, and soon showed his talent in tuning engines to perfection, as well as in the competitive exploits of racing cars and motorcycles in those pioneering days. He also became interested in the early achievements of aviators, and by 1909 had set himself the task of designing and building his own aircraft in Joe's workshop. Eventually he won a £100 prize offered by the Irish town of Newcastle for an aviator to fly over two miles, which he completed on 8 August 1910, thus becoming the first Irishman to design, build and fly his own aeroplane.

In 1913 Harry married Maureen Watson, one of 11 children of a grocer whose shop was in the nearby village of Dromore. The Watson family were also Plymouth Brethren, and needless to say Harry Ferguson's agnosticism did not align well with Maureen's parents. Maureen was to become an abiding support to Harry throughout his tempestuous life, which he always greatly respected. They produced one daughter, Betty.

Around this time Harry became a keen supporter of the Ulster Volunteer Force, whose members numbered 100,000. He became involved in the shipment of guns and ammunition from Hamburg to Larne, which were then secretly brought ashore.

At the start of World War I the Irish government asked Harry Ferguson to supervise the testing of early American tractors bought in to foster home-grown food production. He tackled the work with help from John Chambers, Willy Sands and Archie Greere, who were appalled by the weight and clumsiness of these machines. This gave the small group impetus to develop a better combination of tractor and plough.

Harry Ferguson held the belief that extra trac-

"Old Meets New" in June 1947. In 2007 the driver was 88 years old. Note the single-rib front tyres. Photo supplied by Jim Russell

tion could be gained by mounting the plough directly onto the tractor. His concept evolved slowly and eventually became a workable reality in 1933 with completion of the Black Tractor and its two-furrow plough incorporating three-point hydraulic linkage and Ferguson System draft control - the first of its type in the world. This tractor is now on display at the Science Museum in London.

Over the next 18 months refinements were made to the prototype and working drawings were finalised. Harry Ferguson was then able to approach David Brown of Huddersfield, a renowned firm of gear cutters that had produced gears for the Black Tractor. An agreement was signed to the effect that David Brown would manufacture the tractors and implements, while Harry Ferguson would design and market the finished products. The tractor would be known as the Ferguson Type A, generally referred to as the Ferguson Brown. The first presentation to the public was in the hop gardens of Hereford in May 1936, and by now the paint finish was battleship grey.

By 1939 the relationship between Harry Ferguson and David Brown came to breaking point because the Type A was not selling as well as had been hoped and David Brown saw the need for a bigger tractor. So, with about 1330 units made, production came to an end.

To backtrack slightly to the autumn of 1938, Harry Ferguson had shipped two of his tractors and some implements to Dearborn, USA, so that he could demonstrate their efficiency to Henry Ford and his top engineers; he wisely took along a wind-up demonstration model to enhance the show! Henry Ford was most impressed, and on the strength of what he witnessed, shook hands with Harry Ferguson on a deal whereby Ford would produce a light tractor incorporating Harry Ferguson's patents, while Harry Ferguson would be responsible for design and marketing. Design and development work got under way rapidly with input from Ford and Ferguson engineers, and by 1 April 1939 a prototype tractor was shown to a few special guests. This was to become the basis of a production model, the Ford 9N with Ferguson System, whose production began in June 1939 and ended in 1947 with just over 306,000 units produced.

During World War II hundreds of these tractors were shipped to England under the

SOMETHING HAS HAPPENED...

An early Ford Ferguson brochure contained this picture of Harry Ferguson and Henry Ford discussing their joint creation.

lend-lease scheme implemented by the British government in an attempt to dramatically increase food production. Harry Ferguson had hoped that when hostilities ended the Ford Motor Company of Dagenham would take up construction of Ferguson System tractors, but that did not come about. So he approached numerous other motor manufacturers in England and eventually reached an agreement with John Black of the Standard Motor Company to produce TE20 (Tractor England) tractors at its then-redundant armaments factory in Banner Lane, Coventry. Production was under way by 1946, albeit at a slow rate, with just over 300 made that year; in contrast, production for the whole of 1947 was about 20,580 tractors. It should be reiterated that Harry Ferguson Ltd was a design and marketing organisation, the tractors and their implements being produced by outside engineering subcontracting firms strictly to Harry Ferguson's specifications.

In America Harry Ferguson had in May 1939 formed a company jointly with implement manufacturer Eber Sherman known as the Ferguson-Sherman Manufacturing Corporation, but by 1941 Eber Sherman had resigned from the corporation and the trading title became Harry Ferguson Incorporated. With sales of Ferguson tractors and implements growing steadily in England and abroad, Harry Ferguson turned his attention to setting up his own manufacturing facility on a greenfield site in Dearborn, where a large and well-equipped assembly shop was built to high standards and in record time. Assembly of TO20 (Tractor Overseas) tractors started in 1948, and during that year 1807 units were built; the following year saw 12,852 tractors come off the assembly line.

The next notable episode in Harry Ferguson's life was the court case he brought against the Ford Motor Company of America. This was filed in January 1948 and comprised three claims. The first was that Ford had reduced the value of Harry Ferguson Inc to zero; the claim was for $80 million but under American antitrust law the figure was tripled to $240 million. The second claim, for $11.1 million, was for infringement of Ferguson patents on Ford's 8N tractor. Third was a claim for injuries and damages, with no amount attached. Furthermore, in March 1951 the initial claim of $240 million was raised by Harry Ferguson to $342 million. In April 1952 an out-of-court settlement gave Harry Ferguson $9.25 million. He was disappointed by the amount, but made good publicity of it as representing a victory for the small man, a David and Goliath scenario.

With the lawsuit over, the future of Harry Ferguson Inc looked much more positive. But in the summer of 1952 a steelworkers' strike in the USA, together with one at the Borg-Warner factory (which supplied clutches and gears for the TO20 production line), meant stock soon became depleted. Harry Ferguson Ltd in Coventry came to the rescue by supplying parts to America, and production of TO20s was able to continue; the strike was settled by October. In the meantime, the development office of Harry Ferguson Inc was working on designs for an upgraded TO20, the TO35, which was to be followed by the TO35, launched onto the American market in 1955 under the guiding hand of engineering director Herman Klemm. Overall control of Harry Ferguson Inc was the responsibility of vice president Horace D'Angelo, but the board of directors were not happy people, for sales in 1953 were in decline. Harry Ferguson was keenly aware of this situation, by then a rather tired man and subject to distressing mood swings.

So it was that in July 1953 James Duncan, president of Massey-Harris, visited the works of Harry Ferguson Inc to make an assessment of its operation. This was the beginning of the merger that saw Massey-Harris join with Ferguson to form Massey-Harris-Ferguson, which was announced to the public in a press release on 17 August 1953. Harry Ferguson become the chairman of the new company but for only about a year; discord and internal politics eventually led to him resigning as chairman and he sold his share in Massey-Harris-Ferguson for about $15 million.

He was now free to pursue development work on four-wheel-drive vehicles. Several prototypes were produced by Harry Ferguson Research Ltd, of which some survive to this day. Sadly, none of the major car manufacturers would take on his system.

Massey-Harris-Ferguson thought it prudent to show Harry Ferguson the FE35 (Ferguson England) tractor launched in Britain in 1956, so one was taken to Harry's home at Abbots Wood by long-standing Ferguson employee Bob Annat. Harry Ferguson was highly critical but the occasion led Annat and Ferguson to discuss a dream Harry Ferguson had of designing a light tractor of about 15bhp. The project ultimately came to fruition long after Harry's death in the form of the BMC Mini Tractor (launched in December 1965), which was a design commissioned by BMC from Tractor Research, a branch of Harry Ferguson Research Ltd.

Another project initiated towards the end of Harry Ferguson's life was the P99 four-wheel-drive racing car, a venture prompted by a visit with Peter Warr to Silverstone motor races in May 1960. Sadly, Harry never lived to see the car compete in the 1961 Gold Cup at Oulton Park, driven by none other than Stirling Moss, when it became the first four-wheel-drive car to win a race. Harry Ferguson Research went on to develop and market Formula Ferguson (FF) conversions for road vehicles (including the Jensen FF), and it was finally absorbed into the Ricardo Organisation.

Harry Ferguson's life came to a sad and abrupt end on the morning of Tuesday 25 October 1960, nine days short of his seventy-sixth birthday, when he was found dead in his bath by his wife Maureen. A post-mortem was carried out, and the coroner confirmed that Harry had died of a gross overdose of barbiturate tablets. As requested in his will, Harry's ashes were scattered over Abbots Wood from a light aircraft.

Chapter One

The Beginnings

The MF35's Ancestors: TO30, TO35 and TO40

The genesis of the FE35 (Ferguson England) and the Massey Ferguson 65 (MF65) took place in the design offices of Massey-Harris-Ferguson Detroit. For information on how these designs evolved and were eventually used as the basis for production of the FE35 at Banner Lane in 1956 I have drawn on the extensive knowledge of two American enthusiasts, David Lory and Robert Sybrandy, who kindly supplied me with masses of well-researched text and, most importantly, were happy for me to use their material as the foundation for this first chapter.

The TO30

In the USA, loyal Ferguson users were seeking a more powerful version of the TO20 (Tractor Overseas), which was fitted with a Continental Z-120 petrol engine (120 being the cubic capacity in inches, achieved by having a bore of 3³⁄₁₆in and a stroke of 3³⁄₄in). The compression ratio was 6:1, and bare engine output was 29bhp, with maximum torque of 93lb/ft. In 1949, to meet these users' needs, Herman Klemm, director of engineering at Detroit, instructed his team, headed by chief tractor engineer Nils Lou, to develop a more powerful version, which would be known as the TO30. A pre-production example was shown to Detroit staff in the autumn of 1950, with manufacturing commencing in earnest in August 1951. At first glance the TO30 looked very similar to its predecessor except that the front tyres were now 6.00x16 and the rears 11x28, instead of 4.00x19

and 10x28 respectively.

To gain the required increase in engine output a new Continental petrol engine was installed – the Z-129; again, 129 related to the cubic capacity in inches. The bore was 3¼in and stroke of 3⅜in, with a compression ratio of 6.5:1. These enhancements, together with a change from a flat-topped piston to a cupped version and an improved carburettor, not only boosted bare engine output to 35bhp (with peak torque of 107lb/ft) but also gave improved fuel consumption over the TO20 model. A diesel version of the Z-129 was also developed by Continental, known as the Z-

A brochure produced for the US launch of the TO30, an American upgrade of the original TO20. TO stood for Tractor Overseas.

129D, but there is no evidence that it was ever installed in a Ferguson.

There were other developments to the engine of this model. An improved ball-type governor replaced the earlier TO20 flyweight design. The cooling system pressure was increased from 4psi to 7psi to improve effi-

ciency. Additional lubrication was provided to the centre bearing of the camshaft and the oil filter was relocated on the right-hand side of the engine block, allowing the oil sump to be reduced in depth and in turn increasing ground clearance. This change also eliminated the large hand hole cover in the base of the sump, which was prone to leaks. The flow of oil through the filter was reversed to the pressure side of the pump, thereby greatly improving its filtering characteristics. A new floating oil intake pipe was added to the pump. The Z-120 tooling was modified to produce the Z-129 block, which incorporated the mounting boss for the side-mounted oil filter, as well as cast lugs for mounting the TO30 dynamo.

Other improvements to the tractor followed quite closely the changes that were made to the TE20 over the years of its production in the UK. They included a strengthened clutch, differential and half shafts, and additional oil seals. Improvements to the Ferguson System hydraulic pump included a device to oscillate the control valve to prevent sticking, while gaskets were replaced by O-rings to provide better sealing of the pump side chambers and the lift cylinder to top cover. A cast aluminium spacer was added to the lower end of the lift control fork to aid stability, thus preventing it from separating and disconnecting from the control valve.

The front axle pivot pin was strengthened. The chrome-plated gear lever knob gave way to a large plastic version, and the metal cup at the base of the gear lever was replaced by a rubber boot. The solid step plates gave way to a perforated design, which had much better self cleaning qualities. The PTO shaft remained at 1⅛in diameter, but an annulus was machined at right angles to the splines to allow quick-detach PTO couplings to be used. Optional equipment now included a swinging drawbar with clevis, a PTO extension incorporating the standard SAE 6-spline 1⅜in diameter shaft, a temperature gauge, tractormeter and handbrake.

In 1953 sales of Ferguson tractors fell to 17,314 compared with 35,965 in the previous year - a dramatic decline accelerated by Ford's introduction of a replacement for its 8N, the Golden Jubilee or NAA, which not only boasted an overhead-valve engine but also live hydraulics and optional live PTO.

An early TO35 sales brochure extolling the benefits to users of investing in this new Ferguson.

The TO35

With a new side-mounted baler and forage harvester being prepared for production, Herman Klemm and his team of engineers – including Lee E Elfes, RW King and Ed Zeglen – were working on a new and more powerful tractor, the TO35, to replace the TO30. Klemm had become increasingly frustrated by the repeated delays in the début of Ferguson's long-promised LTX or TE60. He envisaged that a version of the TO35 would be built at Coventry with a diesel engine option, since diesel was

The same brochure, illustrating features of the TO35 including the variable-drive PTO.

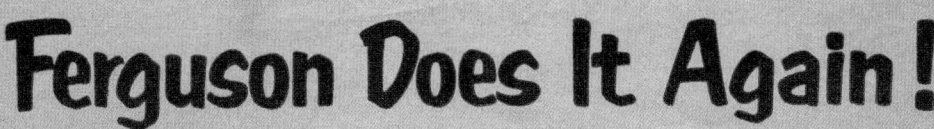

Ferguson Does It Again!

NOW...ONLY THE GREAT NEW

FERGUSON 35

GIVES YOU POSITIVE 4-WAY WORK CONTROL

Quadramatic Control is a new Ferguson exclusive that lets you raise and lower implements, select draft and maintain uniform working depth, adjust the hydraulic system's speed of response, hold implements rigidly at desired position—all with the same quadrant, and with finger touch.

Only the Ferguson "35" gives you so much

Consider these additional "35" features. DEPENDABLE POWER: New supercooled, water-jacketed "wet" cylinder sleeves, plus chrome top rings and improved oil filtration. LOW RPM TORQUE: Engine develops peak torque at only 1,200 to 1,400 rpm. POWER ADJUSTED TREAD: Variable up to 76 inches. RECIRCULATING BALL-NUT STEERING: Reduces shock and kickback, gives smoother performance. JUMBO-SIZE BRAKES: Large, 14-inch, truck-type brakes with special compensating spring to assure even wear. Both pedals on driver's right. TRACTORMETER: Shows rpm's, tractor speed and hours worked. COMPENSATING OVERLOAD RELEASE: Protects both light *or* heavy draft implements.

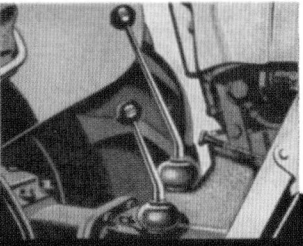

New Dual-range Transmission provides wide range of speeds—6 forward, 2 reverse—to allow you to fit the speed *exactly* to the work, whether you're transplanting, spraying or doing close cultivation in the 35's "creeper" gear. Or plowing or discing in high-range first. Or driving along the highway at rapid transport speeds up to 14 mph.

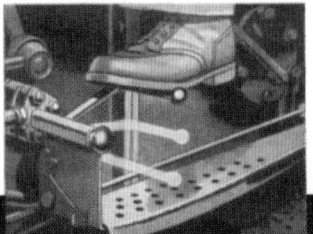

New "2-stage" Clutching controls *both* tractor transmission and PTO with a single pedal for operating such machines as the baler or forage harvester continuously, regardless of tractor starts and stops. Halfway down on the pedal (you don't have to guess, you can *feel* it) disengages the transmission *only*. All the way down stops both transmission and PTO.

The new Variable-drive PTO is no ordinary live power take-off. With the PTO shift you select either the drive that's in ratio to the *ground* speed of the tractor, for such jobs as raking, planting or fertilizing—or, the drive that's in ratio to *engine* speed, for harvesting, foraging, baling or other machine work, demanding continuous PTO operation.

gaining favour in the UK and world markets, but petrol would remain the preferred tractor fuel in the US for a few more years. Planning for the TO35 included maximising the number of interchangeable parts between US- and UK-built tractors, thereby making it possible to source parts or assemblies from either Detroit or Coventry to reduce production costs and to meet fluctuations in demand in either market. Lessons learned during the 1952 Borg Warner strike drove this decision, and the concept would later become a key part of Massey

Ferguson's design and manufacturing policy.

On 10 July 1953 Klemm wrote to Harry Ferguson describing the features of the new TO35 that his team was developing. Harry Ferguson did not like what he read, and ordered Klemm to stop work on the project. He wrote to Klemm on 23 July expressing his disapproval: "Put out of your head that we are going to change the colour of our tractor or its outline. Such talk is disastrous. What is needed is to get our sales organisation on the right basis immediately. The colour of our tractor is right. We did the job with the most extraordinary care so that the machine could run for 10 or 20 years without change".

Klemm was deeply hurt by Ferguson's letter, feeling that Harry Ferguson lacked an understanding of the American market and its need for an updated tractor design. He prepared a 23-page response, explaining the need to proceed with the TO35 design. At this, Ferguson finally relented and allowed Klemm to carry on with the project, in part because Klemm argued that the TO35 was needed to prepare the way for the TE60.

In the event, when the TO35 was launched in the US in January 1955 (a year earlier than planned), it quickly became the standard that other companies had to try to emulate. Acceptance of opinions contrary to his own was not generally one of Harry Ferguson's positive attributes, but in this case his reluctant approval of Klemm's design for the TO35 could be considered one of the best decisions he ever made!

Later, Klemm was asked to re evaluate the TE60, and sent his recommendations to JS Duncan, Massey-Harris-Ferguson president, in a letter dated 10 June 1954. In it he proposed that the TE60 should be shelved in favour of development of a new tractor, the MH70 (though this project did not go ahead). Duncan agreed, and all LTX (TE60) prototypes were scrapped (save one, which escaped for another 20 years). Harry Ferguson was furious but powerless to intervene, and in 1957 he resigned from the board of directors and sold his stock.

The TO35 design included position control and improved draft control, the option of live PTO and hydraulics and a brighter colour scheme – grey for the sheet metalwork and metallic dark green for the main body of the tractor – features that were present on the new Ford Jubilee or NAA model introduced in 1953.

The TO35 had the same general appearance as its precursor the TO30 because the bonnet and grille were almost identical. The horizontal grille louvres were slightly wider than those of the TO30, while the lower front panel was made removable to facilitate installation of a front-mounted auxiliary hydraulic pump to power loaders. The upper section was designed to be easily removed for cleaning the radiator fins. The bonnet retained the tip-up feature but had a centre hinged panel, held by two pushbutton catches, which provided access to the larger (14 US gallon) fuel tank and the radiator filler without tipping the bonnet.

The tractor was initially available in two versions – Standard and Deluxe; a Utility version was added later. The Deluxe model came with a two-stage clutch, providing live PTO and hydraulics. Patents for the dual-clutch listed Lee E Elfes as the inventor. The standard model had a single-stage clutch and therefore no live PTO or hydraulics. To aid recognition the standard version had an S prefix to its serial number. Both types had a variable-drive PTO that allowed the driver to choose between the PTO being driven relative to engine speed or to ground speed; needless to say if ground speed was selected the PTO would rotate anticlockwise when the tractor was travelling in reverse. The patent for the variable drive PTO was registered with Herman Klemm named as the inventor.

All models came filled with the Continental Z-134 petrol engine, which in reality was a slightly enlarged Z-129 unit of 134cu.in, 3⅞in bore and 3⅞in stroke, with a compression ratio of 6.6:1 (a high-altitude version was offered with a compression ratio of 8.1:1). The fact that the pistons and liners from a Z-134 engine could be installed in a Z-129 block was exploited by some users who wished to uprate the power output of their TO30 tractors. The cylinder head used the same valve gear but the head itself was slightly different in that the thermostat was mounted in the water outlet casting instead of in the top radiator hose as on the TO30. The starter, dynamo, voltage regulator and ignition system were all six-volt Delco Remy, as on the TO30.

The front axle carrier was a heavy casting rather than the welded assembly used on the TO30. This casting featured tapped holes both on the underside and at the front, to facilitate the mounting of optional equipment. As the distance between the radiator and the front of

Featuring a new standard of control convenience that lets you FARM MORE . . . WORK LESS . . .

EXCLUSIVE FERGUSON

A later TO35 with Bamboo Beige and Metallic Flint Grey paintwork.

This late-1957 brochure was produced when the colour scheme changed yet again to Metallic Flint Grey for the body with Massey Ferguson Red for the sheet metal work, thus marking the end of the two-line policy.

the engine was greater than on the TO30, an extended shaft on the fan pulley moved the fan close to the radiator. The radius arms and the steering links were the same as on the TO30 but the steering box was of the recirculating ball type, designed to accommodate the power steering system that became a factory-fitted option in late 1955. The engine block casting was modified at serial number 162605 to allow a power steering pump to be installed.

The starter motor was operated by a push-button on the dash via a switch that closed only when the high/low gear lever was in neutral and thus controlled the starter solenoid. The transmission had three forward speeds and one reverse, and was connected to a dual-range epicyclic gearbox controlled by the shorter high/low range gear lever. The slope of the dash panel was more pronounced than on the TO30 and incorporated a tractormeter, oil pressure and water temperature gauges, and an ammeter. An optional clutch pedal stop was available as an accessory to limit clutch pedal travel on live PTO models. This was beneficial when using the tractor on loader work, ensuring that the hydraulic pump continued to operate when the clutch pedal was depressed.

The brake drum diameter stayed the same at 14in but both brake pedals were located on the right-hand side and were provided with a link to connect them together for road work and for parking (a facility that used a spring-loaded paw to engage with a toothed segment). The rear wheel options included the standard 28in rims with 11x28 tyres or power adjustable variable track (PAVT) on 28in rims, or 24in rims shod with 13x24 tyres.

The development of Ferguson System hydraulics led to significant improvements. Draft control through top link sensing now operated in both compression (as before) and tension, this being more successful with light draft implements, and also giving some protection against shock load with heavy implements when travelling in transport mode. This draft control was regulated by the short outer lever of the two lever quadrants; it was also used to give consistent pumping if required. The longer inner lever raised and lowered the lift arms, giving position control, as well as being used to control draft response speed. Patents for these improvements to the hydraulic system listed the inventor as Ernest V Bunting. Initially the lower link levelling box on the right and the connecting link on the left were the same as on the TO30, but in late 1955 at serial number 165750 slightly heavier versions of the components were introduced. Just prior to this, at serial number 161250, the electrical system was changed from six-volt positive earth to 12-volt negative earth.

The TO35 proved to be popular with industrial users, although at first Massey-Harris-Ferguson did not produce a model specifically for that purpose. It did, however, design and market optional pieces of equipment that enabled the TO35 to handle heavy front loaders more effectively. The special heavy-duty front axle kit was introduced in 1956 under part number 677-146. It included a heavier front axle centre section with a stronger pivot bearing and pin, together with reinforced radius arms. Slightly later, a heavy-duty single-stage clutch became available with Ceramet (ceramic/metal) buttons replacing the usual friction material and a heavier pressure plate fitted with stronger springs. Later in 1956 a new version of the TO35 was introduced, known as the Utility. This model featured the above heavy-duty components but was sold without PTO or Ferguson System hydraulics; this reduced the price, but very few survive today.

In May 1956, at serial number 167157, the colour scheme was changed: the sheet metalwork and wheels were finished in Bamboo Beige, while the castings were painted in Metallic Flint Grey to match the then-new Ferguson F40.

Changes were also made to the Continental Z-134 engine at serial number 168505, affecting the camshaft, distributor and carburettors. The Z-129 camshaft (part number 1750-074-MI) had been used in all Z-134 engines prior to this change. Afterwards, engines were fitted with the camshaft of the Z-120 engine (part number 1750-293-MI), but between serial numbers 167258 and 168505 either camshaft was used at random. Once supplies of the Z-129 camshaft had been discontinued the Z-120 camshaft was used as a replacement for all Z-120, Z-129 and Z-134 engines. At this time modifications were made to the springs and weights in the advance mechanism of the Delco Remy distributor. Changes were also made to the Carter carburettor, and in late 1956 approval was finally given for the Marvel-Schebler carburettor to be

used on the Z-134 engine from then on. Both makes could be used, not only on the TO35 but also on the new Ferguson F40 tractors.

At serial number 169566 (mid-1956) the rear axle centre housing was strengthened and the diameter of the studs used to attach the trumpet housings was increased from $\frac{7}{16}$in to $\frac{1}{2}$in. Around this time the thickness of the rear wheel hub bearing retainer and the outer end of the axle trumpet was increased, as was the number of studs holding these parts together, from six to twelve.

At serial number 169567 the construction of the hydraulic lift cover was strengthened, allowing the maximum operating pressure to be increased from 2000psi to 2500psi by the fitment of a stronger relief valve spring. Also at this point the crownwheel to pinion ratio was changed from 6:40 to 6:37. The Ferguson System hydraulic pump was altered at serial number 179304 to a new design with individual valve chambers that could be replaced without changing the whole pump body. Also, the hydraulic lift cylinder diameter was increased from 2½in to 3in and along with this modification the diameter of the bolts was increased from ½in to ⁹⁄₁₆in. On 25 October 1957 the clutch pedal was changed from round to a flat bar with a chequered top, thereby matching the brake pedals.

In December, at serial number 176341, the colour scheme of the TO35 was changed again, this time to Metallic Flint Grey for the main body of the tractor with Massey Ferguson Red being applied to the sheet metalwork and the wheels. This marked the end of the two-line policy, so from then on all tractors and implements were branded Massey Ferguson. Standard and Deluxe versions continued to be available, featuring decals on the sides of the bonnet that read Ferguson 35 or Ferguson 35 Deluxe respectively. At around this time a diesel option became available for both versions. The diesel engine was the Standard 23C imported from Coventry along with some instruments and electrical components; these tractors had side decals that read Ferguson 35 Diesel. The left-hand trumpet housing was modified to provide a bracket mounting point for the second six-volt battery necessary on diesel tractors, and this became standard on all models.

Before long the diesel engine developed a reputation for being difficult to start in cold

The MH50 was available in the following configurations: Row Crop Utility, Row Crop High Arch, Row Crop with twin front wheels and Row Crop with single front wheel. Note the PAVT rear wheels on this example.

weather, so at serial number 188851, in early 1959, glow plugs were fitted to all combustion chambers, replacing the manifold pre-heat of earlier engines. This brought about the desired improvement.

An economy model of the TO35 was introduced around this time. Available only with the petrol engine, the Continental Z-134, it had a single-stage clutch and no ground-speed PTO. The dash had only oil pressure and water temperature gauges, the steering wheel had bare metal spokes, and there was a metal pan seat like the TO20's. To reduce costs the tyre sizes were reduced to 5.50x16 triple-ribs at the front and 10x28 rears. A front weight frame and suitcase (jerrycan) weights became an optional fitment on all models.

On 9 February 1960 the bonnet side decals were changed to read Massey Ferguson MF35 and

the front badge featured the Massey Ferguson triple triangle logo. However, the most significant change was the replacement of the Standard 23C engine with the Perkins A3.152, which had much better cold-starting characteristics. Multi-Power, a Massey Ferguson innovation, was introduced at this stage as an option on live PTO models (for more details, please refer to Chapter Three). Also around this time a differential lock became an optional factory fitment. Fuel gauges were added to diesel models at serial number 209079, but it was not until serial number 209484 that they were fitted to Deluxe petrol variants. Numerous detailed and evolutionary changes continued to be introduced to American-made MF35s until production ended in late 1964.

The San Antonio conference in March 1954 not only resulted in the decision to launch the TO35 a year earlier than originally planned, but it also directed Herman Klemm and his engineers to develop a new model for Massey-Harris dealers. This new model would have different sheet metalwork and the Massey-Harris red colour scheme. It would also be built to accommodate mid-mounted implements and to be available in a tricycle configuration.

The conference named Klemm as the chief engineer for North America, covering both Ferguson and Massey-Harris lines, and directed that the Massey-Harris engineering department should be moved from Racine to Detroit. Not everyone in the Ferguson team was comfortable with the task of designing a tractor for Massey-Harris to compete against their TO35 but on 23 August 1955 it received engineering approval, and by December 1955 the new Massey-Harris 50 was introduced.

The MH50

It is worth considering the MH50 in some detail because it was the MH50 that eventually led to the development of the MF65. Utilising the TO35 skid unit, a new cast pedestal was put in front of the engine, replacing the cast front axle support of the TO35. This lengthened the wheelbase of the tractor and provided attachment points for front-mounted equipment. The new front pedestal eliminated the radius arms and enabled the tractor to be built up as a standard-clearance model, sometimes known as a Utility or Low Clearance. This front end arrangement also enabled the tractor to be built as a high clearance or row-crop model that could accommodate three different front wheel arrangements: wide-track front wheels, dual-wheel tricycle and single-wheel tricycle. The three high-clearance front ends were interchangeable and resulted in a tractor superior to the TO35 for row-crop work.

An additional type of front axle was available. Known as a multi-purpose, it was a heavier, non-adjustable design intended for loader and industrial applications. This new front pedestal was designed to allow a power steering kit to be factory- or field-installed. The steering was controlled by one drop arm from the steering box and one drag link, on the left-hand side of the tractor.

Other changes to the basic TO35 arrangements included placement of the air cleaner forward of the radiator, with the intake through a small grille in the nose cone. The Z-134 engine also featured a new manifold with the silencer mounted above it, which enabled the silencer to be rotated from horizontal to vertical. In the vertical position an upright exhaust pipe could be added. A larger 17 US gallon (14.5 imperial gallons, 37.85 litres) fuel tank was fitted and the bonnet styling and grille mimicked that of contemporary Massey-Harris tractors. Other aspects of the MH50 generally followed the modifications and enhancements introduced over time on TO35 tractors.

The F40

The superiority of the MH50 over the TO35 for row-crop work was immediately apparent, and needless to say Ferguson dealers became incensed that their rivals now had a tractor incorporating Ferguson System hydraulics as well as a fine range of what were basically Ferguson implements. To placate these very real concerns a similar model was introduced for Ferguson dealers in April 1956, known as the Ferguson 40 (F40). It was basically the same tractor as the MH50 but with different styling to the sheet metalwork. A few pre-production examples of this model were painted with grey sheet metalwork and metallic green to the main body of the tractor. By the time the F40 came into production the colour scheme had changed to Bamboo Beige to the sheet metalwork and Metallic Flint Grey to the castings and other parts.

The F40 was available initially with the Continental Z-134 petrol engine in normal and high-altitude types. An LPG version known as the Ferguson 45 was developed but never went into production, although it appears to have been the basis for a later LPG MF50. Standard models had 28in rear tyres, while the Hi Crop (Hi40) had 38in rear tyres. Optional PAVT wheels were available in both sizes, as were all the other accessories for the MH50 and TO35,

A Ferguson F40 tricycle tractor with twin front wheels, PAVT rear wheels and extra work lights on the rear fenders.

An example of a pre-production Ferguson 40, or F40, painted in the green and grey colour scheme. The F40 was basically the same tractor as the MH50 but with slightly different styling to the sheet metalwork.

including a special tractor jack for high-clearance models.

The Ferguson F40 remained in production for only two years, until 1958, at which point the tooling for the bonnet and grille metalwork was shipped to Coventry, where following minor modification it was used to produce the panelwork for the UK-built MF65 in 1958.

In 1958 a new MF50 was produced, senior management having recognised that the two-line policy of marketing was not working. This realisation of the obvious came about as a result of Massey Ferguson commissioning outside consultants McKinsey and Co, who recommended Massey Ferguson should set up distribution of its products through a network of company-owned branches and dealers. To this end Albert A Thornbrough and the new vice president of marketing set out on a seven-month odyssey, travelling across the US in the company's Lodestar aircraft to buy out 17 independent Ferguson distributors and to reduce the number of dealers by 1800. By the autumn of 1957 all but one of the distributors had been bought out at a total cost to Massey-Harris-Ferguson of about $2 million. The only distributor who held out was Southern Tractors of Memphis, Tennessee, who filed an antitrust suit against Massey Ferguson but later settled out of court for $250,000.

The MF50 was developed from the TO35.

For the most part Massey-Harris dealers became the new Massey Ferguson dealers, and as a result of the pruning of dealerships the total number of US and Canadian dealers was reduced from 5700 to 3800. The 53 Massey-Harris sales offices were reduced to 34 branches and eight sub-branches. This leaner, meaner organisation brought about an increase of 30 per cent in US sales and an increase of 9 per cent in Canada on sales in 1958. During this period Massey-Harris tractors were phased out and swift action was taken in late 1957 to introduce the new Massey Ferguson 65.

Before closing this chapter it is worth sharing

SPECIFICATIONS

M·H·F WORK BULL

MODEL 35

SIDE MOUNTED MOWER

- Vibration-Free Counter-Balanced Drive
- 10-Minute Attaching, Detaching
- Shorter Easier Turns
- Cleaner Cutting Around Trees, Stumps
- Faster Sustained Operating Speeds
- Quiet Operation
- Wide Range of Cutting Angles
- Safety Cutter-Bar Release
- Finger-Tip Cutter Bar Controls

Counter-Balanced Drive design makes the Work Bull Side Mounted Mower the most flexible, easily operated mower in the field. Faster, too . . . mowing effectively at speeds of up to 13 miles per hour. Quickly attached, detached, this outstanding Work Bull mower gives you more productive hours and more production per hour.
Counter-Balanced Drive removes cutter bar vibration, reduces noise levels. Better hydraulics, finger-tip controls ease operator's job even more. A wide range of available cutting angles, hydraulic curb lift, safety cutter-bar release make this Work Bull the safest, fastest, most easily operated mower for any heavy-duty mowing application; on highways, for park maintenance, golf courses, airports, landing strips.

See other side of page for more complete details.

M·H·F WORK BULLS
Division of Massey-Harris-Ferguson, Inc.
RACINE, WISCONSIN

M-H-F WORK BULLS pay off as primary equipment . . . as backup machines . . . as utility, cleanup tools

The Work Bull 35 tractor and right-hand-side mid-mounted Dyna-Balance mower, designed for roadside verge trimming in the USA.

The Work Bull 203 and 205, powered by the Perkins A3.152 diesel engine.

David Lory's Turf Special as purchased by him.

some more of David Lory and Robert Sybrandy's contribution that relates to industrial applications of the TO35 models and derivatives. Massey-Harris-Ferguson had close working relations with the Davis brand, who manufactured extremely well-made loaders and backhoes, considered superior to machines made by Wagner, Shawnee and Sherman. In fact, an arrangement to sell Davis equipment through Massey Ferguson branches was established following the break-up of the Ferguson distributor network. In May 1957 Massey Ferguson purchased Mid Western Industries (owners of Davis) at the recommendation of Herman Klemm because Massey Ferguson had a commitment to begin producing industrial equipment, and by buying into this firm development engineering costs would be saved. By July of that year Mid Western Industries had become the industrial division of the US Massey Ferguson Company, based in Wichita, Kansas. Recalling their problems with competing Massey-Harris

The commission plate for the Turf Special.

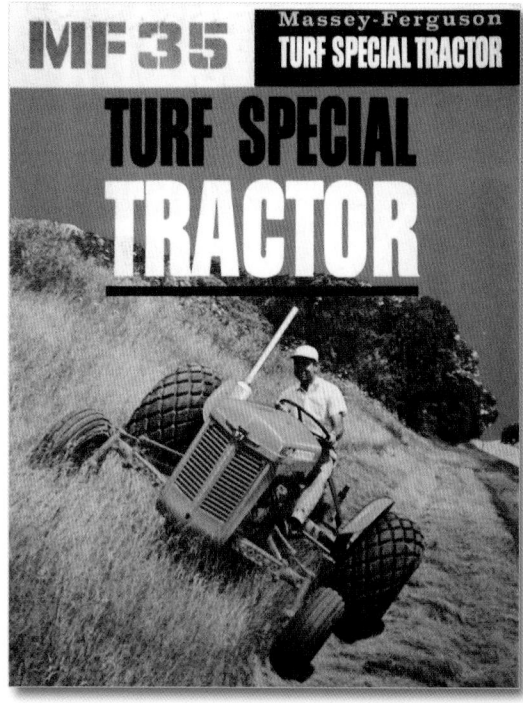

The MF35 Turf Special. Note the wide track setting for extra stability while working across sloping fields.

The right side of the Turf Special

and Ferguson product lines, Massey Ferguson management struggled with integrating this new acquisition into the company. President AA Thornbrough favoured maintaining it as an independent division, while others wanted to integrate it with the agricultural facility. In 1959, while Thornbrough was in the UK attending to other more pressing matters, the dissenters were able to gain influence and succeeded in having the marketing and engineering functions moved to Detroit, leaving only the manufacturing operation at Wichita.

In 1958 Massey Ferguson began producing its first Ferguson-based industrial model, a slightly modified TO35 tractor known as the Work Bull 35, which replaced the TO35 Utility model. It was painted yellow and had the same styling as the TO35 but was fitted with a single-stage heavy-duty clutch and a heavy-duty front axle without radius arms. It was available with or without Ferguson System hydraulics. The Work Bull 35 was powered by the Continental Z-134 petrol engine and was available factory-fitted with a Davis backhoe and loader. Later it was rebranded as the Work Bull 202. A Work Bull forklift was also produced, with the mast assembly supplied by Harlo of Grandville, Michigan. To enable its skid unit to operate the opposite way around from a normal industrial tractor, the mounting of the crown wheel and

pinion in the driving axle was reversed, so the mast became the front of the forklift, with an elevated operator's platform and controls directly behind it. This machine featured a single-stage clutch and was fitted with a mechanical shuttle transmission.

In 1959 a new version of the Work Bull 202 was produced as a result of collaboration between engineers in Detroit and Wichita. It had

The left side of the Continental Z134 petrol engine. Note the oil reservoir for the power steering system fitted to this particular tractor.

This gives a good impression of the overall width and reduced ground clearance of the Turf Special.

David Lory's restored MF35 Utility Government Special alongside a P-51 Mustang.

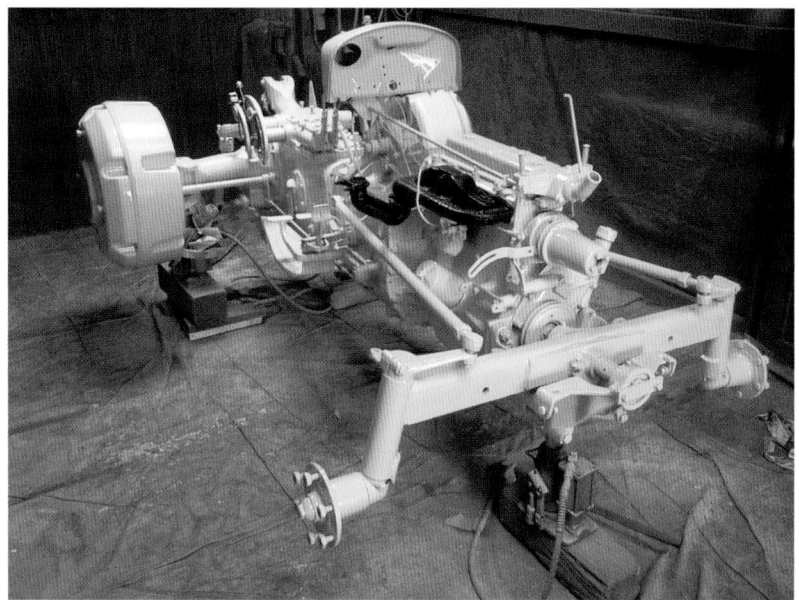

The US Government Special in the paint shop. Note the massive weights on each side of the rear axle, also the heavy duty solid front axle.

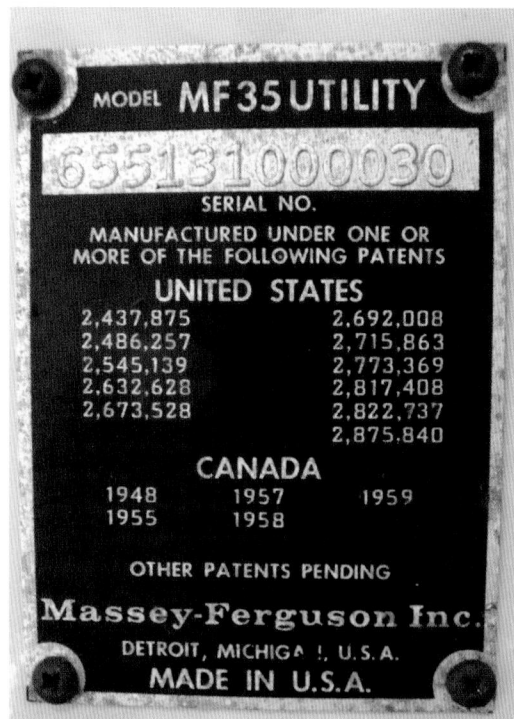

The commission plate of the Government Special.

a rugged new front end that incorporated the loader mounting frame as well as a front-mounted heavy-duty hydraulic pump to power the Davis loader and backhoe. The power steering system used two small independent hydraulic rams to swivel the front wheels. The remainder of the bonnet was of plate steel construction and followed the profile of the front end, which incorporated built-in head-lights. The robust front end in effect formed a

This photograph of the left hand side of the Government Special not only shows the heavy duty front wheels but also the cast steel wheel centres that were a unique feature of these special tractors. Note also the standard rear wheel weight attached to the centre.

This shot shows clearly the two spool valves fitted to these models as well as the Knoedler seat that was not used on any other MF tractors. Note also the bare spokes of the steering wheel, similar to those fitted to early TO20 and TE20 tractors.

heavy-duty bumper. This unit became the basis of an upgraded Work Bull 202 forklift.

Yet another new model was added in 1959, the Work Bull 204, almost identical to the 202 model but equipped with an instant reverse torque converter transmission installed ahead of the main gearbox in place of the clutch. This system is more fully described in Chapter Four. A new Work Bull 204 forklift was based on this unit.

By 1961 two new models were added to the series. The Work Bull 203 was similar to the 202 but fitted with an A3.152 diesel engine and the heavier MF65 rear axle assembly. This model was also available with a manual shuttle transmission and other equipment related to the Work Bull 202.

A full complement of instruments.

The other model introduced was the Work Bull 205, which was similar to the 204 but fitted with a Perkins A3.152 diesel engine and MF65 rear axle; it was fitted as standard with an instant reverse torque converter. The use of this axle gave inboard dry disc brakes, hub reduction gears and a differential lock.

In 1962, when the TO35 became the MF35, a utility version was introduced. Known as the MF35 Utility, it replaced the Work Bull 35 and Work Bull 202. The new model was painted in Massey Ferguson Industrial Yellow and retained a sheet metal bonnet. It naturally had a heavy-duty non-adjustable front axle, without radius arms, and had a foot throttle. The MF35 Utility was available with either single- or double-clutch, and a manual shuttle transmission could be specified. Engine options were either a Continental Z-134 petrol or Perkins A3.152 diesel.

At around the same time another new model was marketed, known as the MF35 Turf Tractor. Similar to the MF35 Utility, it had an adjustable front axle with radius arms, and power steering was optional. It featured smaller-diameter wheels fitted with wide turf tyres on front and rear wheels. Reduced-height mudguards were fitted to match the smaller diameter of the rear wheels. This model could be supplied with or without Ferguson System hydraulics; likewise the PTO. The drawbar was modified to take into account the tractor's reduced height. Again, either the Z-134 petrol or A3.152 diesel engine could be specified.

In 1963 a batch of 170 MF35 government models were specially built for the US air force (USAF). All were fitted with MF65 swinging drawbars, and some also had cabs supplied to Massey Ferguson by Automotive Industries Inc of Owendale, Michigan. The tractors with cabs did not have three-point linkages but were fitted with Ferguson System hydraulic pumps and all the related parts, including a lift cylinder and rocker shafts covered by sleeves over the ends.

It seems likely that these tractors also had two control valves with quick-release couplings. The auxiliary hydraulics and swinging drawbar were used to operate gang mowers needed to deal with cutting large areas of grass economically. All USAF tractors were fitted with the Z-134 petrol engine, a single clutch, manual steering with a bare-spoke steering wheel, a foot throttle, lighting kit and a full set of illuminated instruments that included a tractormeter, oil pressure and temperature gauges, and an ammeter. The electrical system was radio interference-suppressed by the installation of capacitors on the dynamo, regulator and ignition.

The tyre equipment was standard 6.00x16 fronts and 11x28 rears mounted on manually-adjustable wheels. The rear wheel centres were unique to this batch of tractors in that they were made of cast iron, thereby adding weight to aid traction. In addition, they were fitted with an extra standard rear wheel weight to each wheel. The seat was a Knoedler model not used on any other Massey Ferguson tractor, but the seat suspension was the same as that used on late-production MF50 and MF65 tractors. The paint finish was Massey Ferguson Industrial Yellow.

To round off this first chapter, mention must be made of how these tractors or their skid units were sometimes used by outside manufacturers of specialised machines for industrial and forestry applications. The Lev-L-All road grader attachment for the Work Bull 202 or 203 converted the tractor into a fully-functioning long-wheelbase road grader; the front wheels and steering were removed and replaced by the Lev-L-All unit. The Auburn Machine Company's trencher was mounted on the rear of a Work Bull 202 or 203, while often a Massey Ferguson industrial front blade was fitted to aid backfilling.

The MF203 Forwarder was a most unusual looking piece of equipment manufactured by Gafner Machine Co, later known as Gafner Logging Equipment Co. Emil Gafner had started making forestry machines as a Ford dealer in the 1950s. The Iron Mule was one of his creations, involving removal of the front axle of a Ford 600 or 800 series tractor, connecting it to a trailer with an articulating knuckle hitch mechanism, and powering the trailer's axle by a driveshaft connected to the tractor. Hydraulic rams on the articulated hitch were used to steer the machine. A Gafner Hydra-Loader was generally mounted on the rear of the tractor to load or unload logs. Gafner later switched to Massey Ferguson Work Bull models because their heavy-duty front ends and bonnets were much more robust and their rear axles much stronger than those of Ford machines.

Gafner also built other timber loaders and skidders using Massey Ferguson Work Bull tractors as the basis. Massey Ferguson sold the

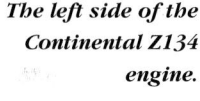

Gafner Iron Mule as the MF203 Forwarder and a later version as the MF2200 Treever.

To conclude, I am deeply obliged to David Lory and Robert Sybrandy for all the information in this first chapter, since it was the TO35 and its derivatives that had an important impact on the demise of TE20 production in Coventry by 1956. Its replacement, the FE35 (Ferguson England), is the subject of the next chapter.

The left side of the Continental Z134 engine.

Part of the publicity material for the MF2200 Treever. Note the new Massey Ferguson Industrial logo in the top left-hand corner, a cross-section of a digger bucket embracing the MF three-triangle trademark.

Chapter Two

Ferguson FE35

Forerunner of the MF35

The Ferguson dealer publication FP658/2M/7/56 *Go Years Ahead with the Ferguson 35 – Our Promotion Plan* was produced in an edition of 2000 copies in July 1956. It was a large format, stiff-covered brochure with a plain grey/bronze finish to the front and back. It told the dealers, with clear and concise wording, how the Massey-Harris-Ferguson organisation would launch the FE35 at a world press announcement on 1 October 1956 at the Grosvenor House Hotel in London, where representatives of the national agricultural and industrial press would be present.

This event was followed by the first public

Cover and first page of an eight-page booklet produced to assist company staff in the fuller understanding of the features and benefits of the then-new model.

viewing, where four of the new FE35s were displayed on high platforms, together with large posters, beside the main roads leading to the World Ploughing Contest and British Ploughing Championships held at Shillingford, Oxfordshire on 10, 11 and 12 October. I was 18 at the time, working as a student on a large mixed farm just 12 miles away, and was taken along to the event by the farm bailiff together with three tractor drivers. I do not remember the four static FE35s, but perhaps we travelled by side roads. I do remember talking to a ploughman who was using a brand new FE35, which smelled new and hot. This tractor made a big impression on me – its striking colour scheme was very much to my liking, as was its robust construction and smooth-running diesel engine. I felt it was a tractor that represented a real and positive development of the TE20 range I had driven on the Oxfordshire farm. Though I did not know it at the time, a similar tractor had been developed and launched in America about 18 months earlier, albeit with a different engine and colour scheme.

A few pre-production FE35s were built up at Banner Lane prior to production starting on Wednesday 22 August 1956, commencing with serial number SDM 1001; this tractor forms part of the display on show at Massey Ferguson's Beauvais facility in France. Six tractors were built on the first day, but it was not until November that production got into its stride.

As far as is known, there is one pre-production FE35 diesel still in existence, at the Coldridge Collection in Devon. It carries a commission plate bearing serial number FE35 003, and its diesel engine is numbered SJ3E. One notable difference when compared to early production diesel models is the presence of a filter fitted to the engine breather on the left-hand side of the engine housing. Early production models had this blanked off, while later models had a modified camshaft cover with no provision for a breather.

As this FE35 003 does not retain its original bonnet or rear mudguards it is impossible to make a comparison with early production tractors. Early publicity photographs showed an open type of Ferguson badge to the front of the bonnet in typical Ferguson script (based on Harry Ferguson's signature), whereas very early on in production it was changed to the familiar solid badge with a chrome border, again in

typical Ferguson script. A Ferguson 35 badge was fitted to either side of the bonnet.

Before discussing the developments incorporated into the FE35 range over its precursor the TE20 it should be pointed out that apart from various engine fuel options – diesel, petrol, TVO and lamp oil – all the tractors were marketed in either basic or Deluxe versions. The basic models had a single-stage clutch, no tractormeter, a pan-type driver's seat and narrow front wheels with 4.00x19 tyres. On the other hand, the Deluxe had a two-stage clutch, which gave the benefit of live PTO with constant-running hydraulic pump when the first stage of the clutch was separated (a great aid for loader

An early sales brochure for the FE35 from October 1956 with Nigel Liney, Ferguson's field test driver, aboard. Note the very early front badge on the bonnet.

the Banner Lane-built tractors followed very similar design and engineering lines apart from the engines that, of course, were all built by the Standard Motor Company at its Canley Road works.

The petrol, TVO and lamp oil engines were all basically upgraded versions of the TE20 spark-ignition unit. Take, for example, the TEA20 petrol engine, which had a bore of 85mm and stroke of 92mm, giving a capacity of 2088cc, with a compression ratio of 5.1:1 and an output 25.4bhp. The FE35 petrol engine had the same 92mm stroke and an enlarged 87mm bore, giving a capacity of 2186cc; with a compression ratio of 5:1 it had an output of 30.5bhp.

The diesel option was a rather different scenario. The Standard 20C diesel installed in the TE20 range was designed in close collaboration with Freeman Saunders, while the head of the 23C engine installed in diesel FE35s had a cylinder head of Ricardo Comet design. Again, it may be worth quoting the comparative dimensions and outputs of these two designs. The 20C engine had a bore of 89.6mm, stroke of 101.6mm, capacity of 2092cc, a 17:1 compression ratio and an output of 25bhp at the belt at 2000rpm. The 23C engine had a bore of 84.14mm and stroke of 137.89mm to give

An early FE35 front bonnet badge, with the later version more generally used below it.

work). It also featured a tractormeter, a cushioned seat squab with a low upholstered backrest, and wider front wheels with 6.00x16 tyres. Tractors were available as Agricultural, Industrial and Vineyard types. No narrow version was offered, as had been the case in the TE20 range.

As outlined in the chapter on the TO30/35,

The front cover of a glossy German brochure dated November 1957; note the front drawbar and the raised air intake.

FE 35 SPEZIAL

1. Dieselmotor mit Einspritzpumpe modernster Konstruktion
2. Druckumlauf-Kühler
3. Kraftstofftank
4. Abgefederte Wartungsklappe
5. Fliehkraft-Olbad-Luftreiniger
6. Wirbelkammer
7. Auswechselbare Zylinderlaufbuchsen
8. Aluminiumlegierte Kolben
9. Rotierende Auslaßventile
10. Dynamisch ausgewuchtete Kurbelwelle

11. Völlig in sich abgeschlossenes Druck-Schmiersystem
12. Neuartiges Kugelwälzlenkgetriebe
13. Zweistufenkupplung mit 2 getriebenen Scheiben
14. Getriebeeingangswelle
15. Zapfwellenantriebe und Pumpe für Hydraulik
16. Getriebe-Vorgelegewelle
17. 3-Gang-Getriebe mit Planetenuntersetzungsgetriebe für 6 Vorwärts- und 2 Rückwärtsgänge
18. Planetengetriebe mit Untersetzung von 4 : 1 in allen Gängen
19. Gangschalthebel

20. Gruppenschalthebel
21. Hydraulikpumpe
22. Gestänge und Nocken der Hydraulik mit folgenden Funktionen :
   a) Heben und Senken des Anbaugestänges
   b) Positionskontrolle
   c) Reaktionsregelung
   d) Zugkraftkontrolle
   e) Überlast-Auslösung
   f) Hydraulische Kraft für zusätzlich angeschlossene Druckzylinder
23. Bedienungshebel der Hydraulik

24. Zugkraftkontrollhebel
25. Kontrollfeder mit Zugkraftregelung bei Druck- und Zugbelastung
26. Zapfwellenanschluß (34,9 mm)
27. Zapfwellenschaltgetriebe für motor- oder gangabhängige Schaltung der Zapfwelle
28. Robustes Differentialgetriebe
29. Nach hinten umklappbarer Stahlkübelsitz mit Schaumgummisitz und -rücklehne
30. FERGUSON-Dreipunkt-Aufhängung
31. FERGUSON-Traktometer
32. Sicherheits-Startschalter

A magnificent cutaway of the FE35 from the same German brochure – fine if you can read German!

Left side view of the Standard 23C diesel engine installed in a Vineyard FE35.

The Standard 23C diesel engine clearly showing the CAV ditributor type injection pump.

2259cc, a 20:1 compression ratio and 35.9bhp at the belt with the engine running at 2000rpm.

In the transmission system, for the first time a dual-stage clutch was fitted as standard on the Deluxe range of models. This had the distinct advantage that the forward movement of the tractor could be stopped by depressing the clutch pedal through half of its travel, at the same time enabling the hydraulic pump and engine-driven PTO to continue running. Both the basic and Deluxe versions had the SAE standard six-spline 1⅜in diameter PTO shaft, a move away from the TE20's oddball size of 1⅛in. Both ranges of FE35 tractors had a three-position PTO

The Thermostart fitted to the air intake of diesel FE35s as a cold starting aid. By turning the starter key on the dash to the heat position the element was heated and a valve opened to allow a small quantity of fuel to enter which after a few seconds ignited, thus warming the incoming air.

control lever on the left-hand side of the transmission housing, giving a selection of engine-driven, neutral or ground speed-related operation, which gave about 19in (482mm) of forward travel for one revolution of the PTO.

The gearbox was totally different for the FE35 to bring it more into line with expectations of the day. It gave six forward and two reverse ratios. This was achieved by passing the drive through a 'box with three forward speeds and one reverse. The gears used were straight-cut, sliding mesh, whereas the TE20 had helical-cut gears. The main gearbox was operated by one lever in the conventional manner. The output end of this gearbox was mated to an epicyclic reduction unit controlled by its own shorter lever alongside the main gear lever. This short lever had three positions – high, neutral and low; the neutral position incorporated a switch in the starter solenoid circuit that closed only when in neutral, so that it was not possible to operate the starter with the tractor in gear – a continuation of the safety feature used on the TE20. From the output shaft of the epicyclic unit, drive was taken via a hollow shaft known as the shear tube, which was specially engineered to shear if it became excessively overloaded, thus saving other more expensive components from being damaged.

The rear axle casing was strengthened and more bolts used to secure the trumpet housings to the transmission casing. Although early FE35s still only had six bolts each side securing the half shaft bearings to the outer end of the trumpet housings, this was soon upgraded to 12 bolts per side. This increase in strength was necessary not only to cope with the increased engine power, but also to deal with the increased lifting capacity of the hydraulic linkage and the heavier implements that became available for the FE35.

The pedals for the independent brakes were located side by side on the right of the transmission housing and could be latched together for road use, slight discrepancies in brake wear being compensated for by stout coil springs within the operating rods. A safety parking latch to hold the pedals in the depressed position was provided.

Probably the most significant engineering development on this FE35 range over its precursors was the availability of both Ferguson System draft control and the more basic position

control. This necessitated the use of two control levers mounted in separate quadrants but adjacent to each other. The inner lever raised and lowered the implement and held it in any desired position, while at the lower end of its arc it became a response control selector when operating in draft mode. The outer lever controlled the draft and in turn the depth of tillage implements. It was also used to control the hydraulic output from tappings mounted either side of the hydraulic cover. Also mounted on top of this cover was a removable plate known as the transfer cap, which could be taken off and replaced with an isolator valve, used to cut off the flow of oil to the main lift cylinder within the tractor and then supply oil to an external device. The operation of the top link sensing was developed so it would operate in either compression (as was the case on the TE20) or in tension, beneficial for heavy overhanging implements and for light cultivation.

At the front of the FE35 the front axle support was strengthened, made of malleable iron, and

A nearside view showing the stout compression spring incorporated in the brake linkage as well as the PTO lever, shown in the neutral position. Moving the lever upwards engages PTO relative to engine speed, and lowering it gives PTO relative to ground speed.

A nearside view of the FE35 diesel Vineyard model. The cutaway to the lower side bonnet panels enables the steering drag link arms to clear when the front axle articulates.

A general view of the dash panel of a De Luxe diesel FE35. It also shows the longer main gear lever and the shorter one controlling the High-Start-Low ratios.

Offside of the FE35 Vineyard model. The exhaust passes below the footplate.

The hydraulic control quadrants are mounted either side of the seat; just below the quadrant on the right is the hydraulic transfer cap.

This head-on view emphasises the narrow track of the Vineyard model.

A rear view showing the extended handle to the levelling box.

The sets to the radius arms and steering drag links are visible here.

had provision for an underside location pad, with five deeply drilled and tapped holes for the attachment of front implements or a weight frame. Likewise four similar holes were provided under the bellhousing for the attachment of implements such as a mid-mounted mower or front-end loader. These holes were tapped to ⅝in UNC.

The front axle followed the same basic layout as the TE20's but was made of slightly heavier sections. The Ferguson-patented double drag link steering system was retained so that track width adjustments could be made without altering the steering geometry. The one component of the steering system that was radically redesigned was the steering box; it still featured the double drop arm layout but with the left-hand drop arm slightly shorter than the right. The steering box was a screw and recirculating ball nut unit with the nut supported on the threaded end of the steering column. As the steering wheel was turned, the nut ran up and down the threaded section, taking with it a

An FE35 Industrial fitted with a MF737 Fork Lift made under licence by Fewsters of Stocksbridge, Northumberland.

toothed segment integral with the left-hand output shaft. The toothed segment on the right-hand side engaged with the upper face of the left-hand segment. This explains the differences found in the length of the drop arms. It proved to be a very low-friction design and was claimed to reduce kickback, a feature that at times rather spoilt the steering on the TE20.

A new look for the tractor was obviously intended to give the impression of workmanlike efficiency and rugged build quality. The striking metallic bronze paint finish to the main body of the tractor was set off by traditional Ferguson light grey for the wheels and sheet metal. The bonnet was made to hinge forward as on the TE20 but the angle of tip was reduced. Everyday servicing of fuel and coolant was via a hinged

4 MAIN FEATURES *which provide complete*

New
Hydraulic System

The famous Ferguson system that has more than proved itself is now even better ! The unique double quadrant offers "finger-tip" control of all front, mid and rear mounted machines.

New
Power Take-off

With the new 35 you have the choice of two different power take-off drives. Select a drive that's in ratio to engine or ground speed—and you have a P.T.O. drive to suit a host of jobs !

New
Dual Clutch

The Ferguson 35 De Luxe is fitted with Dual Clutch which makes your "Engine Speed" P.T.O. live—that means a running P.T.O. (even though the tractor is stationary) for mechanically propelled attachments. Further, this unique Dual Clutch ensures a constant running hydraulic pump–a boon for loaders !

New
6-speed Gearbox

An amazing range of speeds can be obtained from the Ferguson 35 ! There are no less than six forward and two reverse gears—a gear and a speed for every job. Creep as slow as 0.3 m.p.h. or speed up to 14 m.p.h. for fast jobs. Never before such a selection of gears for so much work !

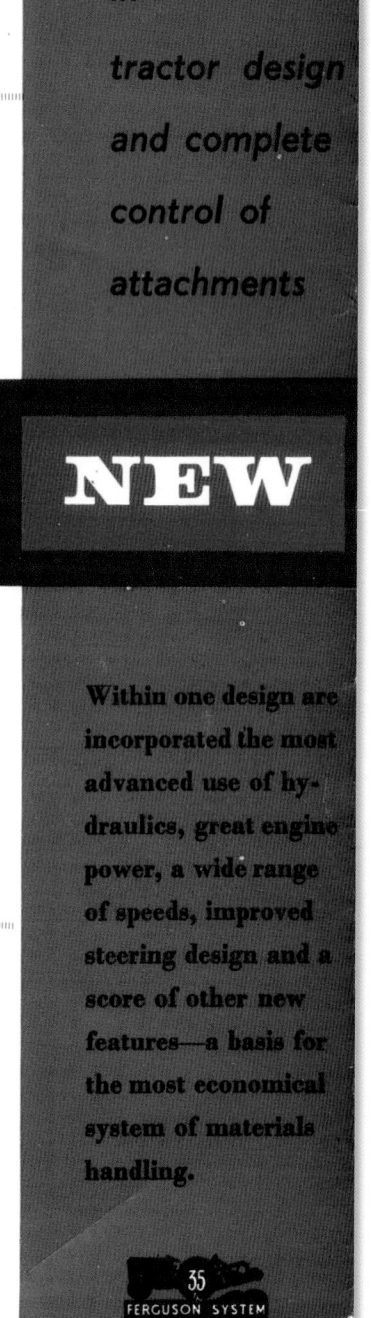

SELECTIVITY and **FLEXIBILITY** in tractor design and complete control of attachments

NEW

Within one design are incorporated the most advanced use of hydraulics, great engine power, a wide range of speeds, improved steering design and a score of other new features—a basis for the most economical system of materials handling.

This sales brochure for the FE35 Industrial model is dated March 1957.

panel mounted centrally along the bonnet. These early FE35 tractors had a pair of chrome push buttons fitted to open this panel. Another new feature was the fitting of a quickly removable radiator grille to facilitate easy cleaning of the radiator fins, and it was possible as optional equipment to replace the grille with a chaff screen.

On Deluxe models a tip-up, hinged, cushioned seat was standard, complete with a low

The Fork Lift hydraulic controls and tilt ram.

padded back support. Footboards were standard so a driver could stand or sit as necessary. Also featured for the driver's convenience on Deluxe models was a dash-mounted tractormeter, which indicated hours worked at 1550rpm engine speed. It was calibrated in miles per hour for each gear ratio, and belt and PTO operation speeds were marked. The only other instruments installed were an oil pressure gauge on all models, and an ammeter on diesel models only. Petrol, TVO and lamp oil models were also equipped with a coolant temperature gauge on both standard and Deluxe models.

Model variants were offered for a wide range of uses, not only in agriculture but also for municipal and industrial purposes. They were made available very early on once production was under way at Banner Lane. Obviously, what was saleable in TE20 days would continue to be in demand for the next generation of tractors, so it was prudent for Massey-Harris-Ferguson to be producing these variants at an early stage.

The Agricultural FE35 was manufactured in very small numbers in a Vineyard configuration whereby the front track was reduced to 37in (940mm) and the wheelbase was extended slightly to allow the front wheels to clear the bonnet on full lock. This was achieved by having a much reduced set-back to the shortened front axle. To keep the centre of gravity within bounds and to ensure the tractor remained reasonably stable, smaller front and rear wheels were fitted, tyre sizes being 5.00x15 on the front and 9.00x24 on the rear. This gave a drawbar height range of 8in (203mm) to 21in (533mm), whereas a standard FE35 had a range of 10in (254mm) to 23in (584mm). As a result of the reduced wheel diameter the top speed was slower, at 12.68mph (20.4kph).

Another modification necessary because of the greatly reduced width was the relocation of the draft and position control quadrants to either side of the seat, the draft control lever being on the left, the position control lever on the right; on these models there was no adjustable sector on the draft control lever quadrant. The lift arms were made to an almost straight form because of the restricted width between the mudguards. Likewise it was not possible to mount one of the six-volt batteries on a bracket positioned to the left of the driver, and it was relocated on a mounting bracket towards the rear of the engine on the left-hand

side – a rather untidy arrangement – while the second battery remained under the bonnet just in front of the dashboard.

The supplement issued with FE35 Vineyard variants in addition to the standard instruction book made it clear that front wheel weights of 90lb (41kg) were highly recommended and that the three-ton Ferguson trailer could be operated providing the wheel track of the tractor did not exceed 56in (1422.4mm) and that the trailer's axle was set in the forward position. A specially-modified Ferguson jack was made available for these models.

For the Industrial version of the FE35 the modifications necessary to make the tractor comply with the Road Traffic Act of 1947 followed very similar lines to those adopted on earlier TE20 models. Standard equipment on

The correct location of the Lucas HF horn fitted to Industrial models.

Industrial FE35s included heavy-duty industrial tyres front and rear, a high-frequency horn mounted adjacent to the timing cover on the left-hand side of the engine operated by a push-button on the instrument panel, and a driving mirror to the right-hand side of the panel.

The braking arrangement was modified by the fitting of two sets of concentric brake shoes within a wider drum, still of 14in (355.6mm) diameter. The inner pair was 1½in (38mm) wide and was operated mechanically either by the handbrake lever mounted on the top left-hand side of the transmission housing or by independent brake pedals mounted either side of the transmission housing. It should be remembered that both independent brake pedals on Agricultural models were situated on the right-hand side of the gearbox. The other pair of brake shoes was 2in (50mm) wide and of two leading shoe design, with each shoe being operated by its own hydraulic cylinder. This arrangement gave very efficient braking in the

forward direction, but very poor performance in reverse. The master cylinder was on the left-hand side of the transmission housing, and the brakes were operated by a single foot pedal on the right; the clutch pedal remained on the left.

The optional front bumper the full width of the tractor was mounted on two strong compression springs to absorb impact. Also available as accessories were front and rear fenders, wide enough to extend beyond the width of the tyres and thus affording good protection for the driver. Rear weights were offered for users requiring added traction. These were attached inside the wheel centres by special bolts and each weighed 120lb (54.5kg); two per wheel could be added if necessary. It should be mentioned that Industrial FE35s were often expected to operate non-Ferguson equipment.

All in all the FE35 range proved most popular with farmers and others who appreciated the extra power and wider range of gear ratios that were available on this Ferguson System tractor.

The standard 500 x15 front tyre and wheel assembly of a Vineyard FE35.

Front mudguards were generally fitted on the Industrial models.

Front wheel weights (left) were absolutely necessary when using the Fork Lift, as here on the industrial model.

Chapter Three

The MF35

The grey and bronze colour scheme ran until 1957, when the colours were changed to Red and Metallic Flint Grey at serial number 74656. The MF65 MkI, first produced in December 1957, was finished in the same colours. Mechanically the MF35 was unchanged from the FE35, and even the bonnet badges were still Ferguson until the introduction of the three-cylinder Perkins type A3.152 diesel engine on serial number 166596. There was another change to the bonnet at this point, when the press-button release for the top lid was replaced by smarter centrally-mounted turn-clips. Changes were also made to the power output and to the colour of the paintwork, with Massey Ferguson Red for the sheet metalwork and Stoneleigh Grey for the tractor's body and wheels.

Massey Ferguson acquired the engine manufacturer F Perkins of Peterborough in 1959, and just prior to that had taken over the Standard Motor Company's manufacturing facility at Banner Lane, Coventry. The Standard 23C diesel engine had built itself a reputation as a bad starter in cold weather despite several subtle cylinder head modifications, including a head fitted with individual heater plugs in each combustion chamber, which became optional for cold climates. Just to compare the outputs of the two engines, the 23C developed

This new Triple Triangle bonnet badge arrived with the MF35 tractors in November 1957.

An MF35X Vineyard model fitted with an MF723 Post Hole Digger.

This offside view of the MF35X Vineyard model illustrates the sets in both then radius arms and the drag links necessary because of the tractor's narow width.

The MF35X Vineyard seen from the front.

34bhp from 2259cc at 2000rpm, while the Perkins A3.152 produced 37.3bhp from 2500cc at the same revs – both figures measured at the PTO.

At the point of change to the three-cylinder Perkins engine the concept of Standard and Deluxe models was dropped in favour of what was a better equipped tractor – all now featured a cushioned seat and tractormeter, but the option of either single or dual clutches

Nearside of a MF35X Vineyard tractor; note here the cutaway to the lower side of the bonnet to allow clearance of the drag links.

remained in place. The choice of fuels was as before, the most popular being diesel, followed by TVO and petrol; lamp oil engines were only available for export markets. The basic model range remained the same, consisting of Agricultural, Vineyard and Industrial; there was no narrow version.

The next improvement was the introduction of the MF35X on 8 November 1962 at serial number 302413. The major development was

MF35 petrol model finished in MF Red and Stoneleigh Grey. The decals on the bonnet side are not quite correct. This is not a 35X and the Ferguson System logo should have the tractor facing forward!

Unusual today: a petrol-engined version of the MF35. Note that the Ferguson System logo faces the wrong way and the fact that petrol models were not designated 35X — the X referred to the uprated Perkins A3.152 diesel engine.

The other side of the petrol MF35, showing the carburettor and induction manifold.

Possibly an early MF35X; note the unusual mid-mounted implement.

The Zenith 28G updraught carburettor as fitted to the MF35 petrol model.

An MF35X Multi-Power with the full-length safety fenders fitted for health and safety requirements.

The same tractor with the sheep showing great interest in our photographer!

the enhanced power output from the diesel engine, which went up to 41.5bhp at the PTO at 2250rpm engine speed. Also introduced was the option of a differential lock but there is evidence that some late MF35s were also fitted with this system. The raised air intake through the bonnet introduced towards the end of MF35 production was continued on to the MF35X, a feature that was standard even on the bronze and grey FE35s for some export markets. Very early MF35X tractors still retained the shell-type rear fenders with tapered foot-plates but they were soon replaced with full-length safety fenders, which bolted directly to the new rectangular footplates.

Apart from the increase in power from the engine, probably the most significant feature was the availability of Multi-Power (a form of

New improvements have raised the output of this famous three cylinder engine to 44 h.p. without any lessening of fuel economy. The new rated speed of 2250 r.p.m. has still further widened the interval between torque peak and maximum power. Such immense torque 'back-up', over a range of nearly 1000 r.p.m., is supremely valuable in a tractor engine. It enables the engine to 'hang-on' to increasing loads when soil resistance builds up against an implement. In practice it means great time saving because you can pull through the tough spots without having to change down.

The A3-152X will give you years of reliable service. Here are just a few of the quality features in its design . . . crankshaft supported on four main bearings; highly sensitive mechanical governor — built in to the precise distributor-type fuel pump; efficient, easy to service twin fuel filters; combined direct and indirect injection for sure starting and clean burning to get the most out of every ounce of fuel. This is the engine for the kind of year-in, year-out work that puts greater profit into farming.

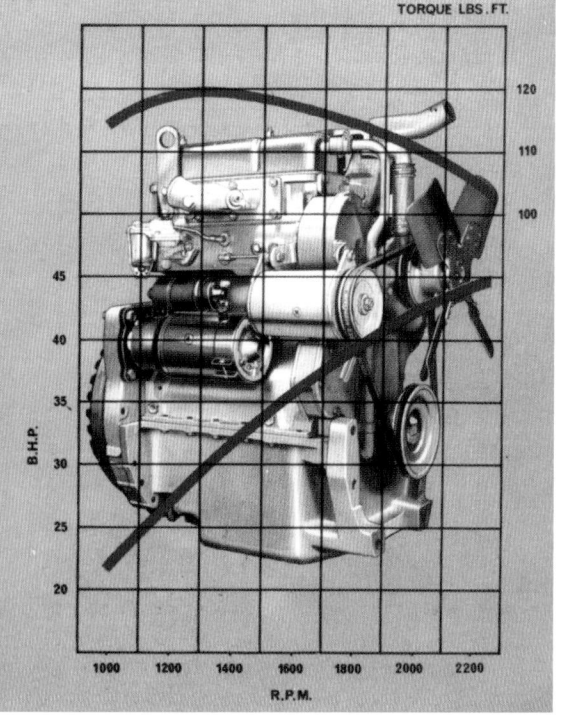

An MF brochure dated December 1962 highlighting the improved Perkins A3.152 diesel engine. This image still shows the non-X engine – it has two brackets securing the dynamo; a true X engine has a one-piece mounting bracket

This instructional poster explained the workings of Multi-Power.

MASSEY - FERGUSON
MULTI-POWER *12 SPEED* TRANSMISSION

This early MF brochure dated December 1962 extols the benefits of Multi-Power, an ingenious transmission system that doubled the number of gears available.

MASSEY-FERGUSON **35 X** TRACTOR with **MULTI-POWER**

'flick-change' transmission

overdrive) as an option on dual-clutch models. Multi-Power was unique to Massey Ferguson at the time, although at a later date Ford introduced Dual Power (underdrive), a similar and arguably safer system since Ford's design gave the driver engine braking in both high and low ratios, while Multi-Power only afforded engine braking in high.

Multi-Power gave the driver the facility to shift a gear ratio on the move and under power, but only from high to low or vice versa, not between manually-selected gear ratios. Multi-Power worked by driving the gearbox counter shaft at one of two selected

The dash-mounted Multi-Power control lever.

The tip-up seat of an MF35. You paid extra for a padded seat.

A close-up of the Perkins A3.152 engine. The Ferguson decal is misplaced. Note the 35X-type one-piece dynamo mounting bracket.

The swing drawbar was still an optional extra.

ratios, thus giving twelve forward and four reverse speeds. To achieve this, additional components were needed, which basically comprised: a constant running and dedicated small hydraulic pump to power the hydraulically controlled multi-plate clutch pack; a hydraulic control valve situated within the bellhousing with a mechanical linkage protruding through the top connected to a control lever mounted on the right-hand side of the dash panel; and a differential clutch coupler, a mechanism that worked in a similar way to the Bendix drive fitted to some simple starter motors. Multi-Power tractors could not be tow-started.

The maximum speed of an MF35X without Multi-Power on 11x28 rear tyres was 16.4mph at 2250rpm, whereas with Multi-Power fitted and set in the high position a top speed of just over 21.7mph was achieved at the same engine speed.

So here we had a model that supplied the user with a useful number of features. As well as having a choice of single- or dual-clutch, the buyer could specify Multi-Power (giving twelve forward speeds) or opt for the standard six-speed gearbox. To tailor the tractor more exactly to users' needs the following optional equipment was developed: a full lighting set, an automatic pick-up hitch, a swinging drawbar,

An illustration of the standard Industrial MF35X.

An experimental Industrial MF35. It has obviously seen a lot of service while in use at Banner Lane.

It is fitted with a Ford Dexta F3 engine; note the traces of Ford blue paint.

The dashboard and throttle quadrant, but why the blanked off hole? Was this for a coolant temperature gauge?

front and rear wheel weights, power adjustable rear wheels, a dual rear wheel kit and a rear-mounted belt pulley. There was also the option of dual category I and II lower linkage ends; needless to say very few were sold.

With production for the year 1963 reaching 45,023 units it is not surprising Massey Ferguson ensured that specialist users were well catered for, as had been the case with previous models, the MF35X being offered in both Vineyard and Industrial versions. These were covered in Chapter Two, and as far as I am aware they remained current. Production of all models ended in 1964 at 388,382, having started in 1956 at 1001, so in the nine-year period of production 387,381 units were produced. The good old days of real British industry!

The Ford Perkins F3 diesel engine as fitted to the Ford Dexta tractor, i.e. the engine fitted to the tractor shown opposite. I painted it in Stoneleigh Grey so that it did not look out of place in the Coldridge Collection.

You have been warned!

Chapter Four

The MF65

The new MF65 was launched in November 1957, fitted with the Perkins A4.192 diesel engine.

To trace the genesis of the MF65 it is worth returning to the era of Harry Ferguson. In the early 1940s, Ford-Ferguson engineers produced five prototypes of a scaled-up Ford 9N. One of these machines, numbered P4, was shipped to Fletchampstead Highway, the development office of Harry Ferguson Ltd, in 1948 to be used as a backdrop to the development work that was about to start on the Ferguson, Large Tractor Experimental, LTX (see *Ferguson TE20 In Detail*, Chapter 13).

Although the TE20 range was selling extremely well, not only in Britain but in world markets, there was a growing need for a more powerful tractor incorporating all the benefits of the Ferguson System. Development of five LTX

The Perkins A4.192 diesel engine fitted in the MF65. Note the wedge-shaped casting between the sump and the bell housing, an easy way to identify the MkI model.

A cutaway of the MF65 MkI.

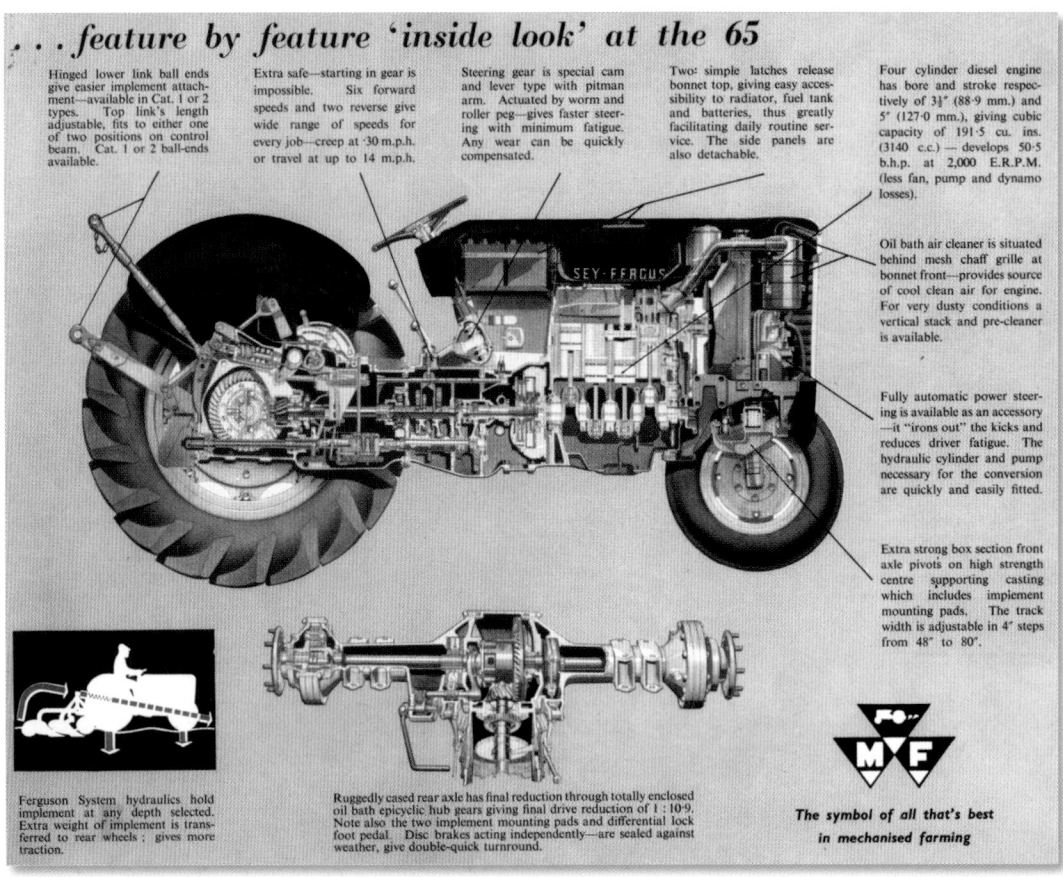

. . . *feature by feature 'inside look' at the 65*

Hinged lower link ball ends give easier implement attachment—available in Cat. 1 or 2 types. Top link's length adjustable, fits to either one of two positions on control beam. Cat. 1 or 2 ball-ends available.

Extra safe—starting in gear is impossible. Six forward speeds and two reverse give wide range of speeds for every job—creep at ·30 m.p.h. or travel at up to 14 m.p.h.

Steering gear is special cam and lever type with pitman arm. Actuated by worm and roller peg—gives faster steering with minimum fatigue. Any wear can be quickly compensated.

Two: simple latches release bonnet top, giving easy accessibility to radiator, fuel tank and batteries, thus greatly facilitating daily routine service. The side panels are also detachable.

Four cylinder diesel engine has bore and stroke respectively of 3½″ (88·9 mm.) and 5″ (127·0 mm.), giving cubic capacity of 191·5 cu. ins. (3140 c.c.) — develops 50·5 b.h.p. at 2,000 E.R.P.M. (less fan, pump and dynamo losses).

Oil bath air cleaner is situated behind mesh chaff grille at bonnet front—provides source of cool clean air for engine. For very dusty conditions a vertical stack and pre-cleaner is available.

Fully automatic power steering is available as an accessory —it "irons out" the kicks and reduces driver fatigue. The hydraulic cylinder and pump necessary for the conversion are quickly and easily fitted.

Extra strong box section front axle pivots on high strength centre supporting casting which includes implement mounting pads. The track width is adjustable in 4″ steps from 48″ to 80″.

Ferguson System hydraulics hold implement at any depth selected. Extra weight of implement is transferred to rear wheels ; gives more traction.

Ruggedly cased rear axle has final reduction through totally enclosed oil bath epicyclic hub gears giving final drive reduction of 1 : 10·9. Note also the two implement mounting pads and differential lock foot pedal. Disc brakes acting independently—are sealed against weather, give double-quick turnround.

MF

The symbol of all that's best in mechanised farming

A pre-production example of the Ferguson TE60, as it was to be known, on the left alongside a Ferguson FE35. The man standing on the right is believed to be Billy Beatty, who came over from Northern Ireland, with Alex Patterson who was in charge of the engineering development workshop. Note the other field prototypes in the background and the Massey Harris Pony tractor. I wonder what else lurks behind the white sheet?

prototypes, three with petrol engines and two with diesel, was put in hand in 1948 in strict secrecy. In my archives I have a copy of the full specification of the production diesel model that emerged from these prototypes, to be known as the TE60, rated at 56bhp at 2000rpm. The document is dated 8 October 1953. Also to hand are copies of a dealers' order book listing customers who had signed up to buy this larger model when production began – a clear indication of how close this tractor came to being a reality.

Just prior to the merger of Ferguson with Massey-Harris in early August 1953, Harry Ferguson set up a demonstration involving the LTX ploughing up and down a sloping field that had been heavily coated with farmyard manure during the previous day. To add to the drama Ferguson made sure he had a Massey-Harris 744 working alongside. This demonstration was in the presence of James Duncan, president of Massey-Harris, and other top staff. Jack Bibby, the factory test driver, was driving the Ferguson LTX, which with the benefits of draft control and a special fingertip-controlled differential lock ran rings around the MH744; there was no

The finest 50 h.p. class tractor . . . the M-F 65

The front cover of an early MF65 sales brochure.

comparison. Sadly, whether for reasons of ego or politics we do not know, at a crucial product policy meeting that took place in San Antonio, Texas between 6 and 11 March 1954, North American sales staff decided they were not

The new MF65 MkII. Note the full complement of front weights and the wider front and rear track settings

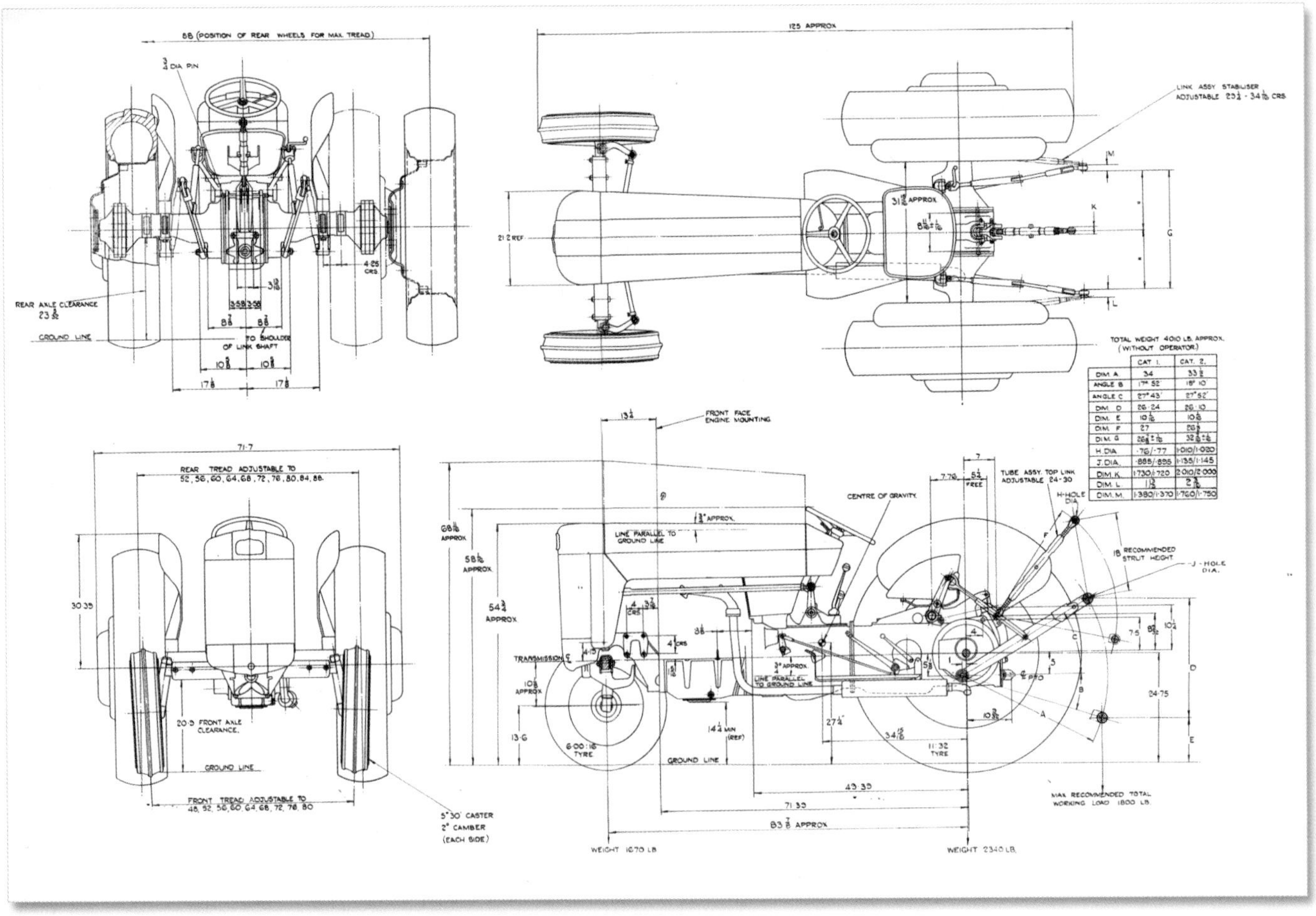

	CAT. 1	CAT. 2
DIM. A	34	33½
ANGLE B	17° 52′	18° 10′
ANGLE C	27° 43′	27° 52′
DIM. D	26.24	26.10
DIM. E	10½	10½
DIM. F	27	28½
DIM. G	30¾/14½	32¼/14½
H DIA.	.76/.77	1.010/1.030
J DIA.	.886/.896	1.135/1.145
DIM. K	1.730/1.720	2.010/2.000
DIM. L	1½	2¾
DIM. M	1.380/1.370	1.760/1.750

This dimensioned drawing of the MF65 is taken from MF Dealers Publication Specification and Performance Release S.P.R.89.

The power steering – optional on the MF65 – takes its drive from the timing gears, directly below the injector pump.

impressed with the LTX on the grounds that it lacked the option of a tricycle wheel layout for the specialist row-crop market, and that if a conversion was developed it might appear crude.

James Duncan left it to Hermann Klemm, director of engineering, to have the final say on whether the TE60 should be produced at Banner Lane alongside MF35s or whether a larger tractor (ie the MF65) should be made by using as many parts from the existing MF35 as possible – the Meccano method, as it has been dubbed. This was the route chosen, on cost-saving grounds, and it led to the manufacture of the MF65 MkI, to be followed later by the slightly more powerful MF65 MkII. In November 1957 full technical details of the long-awaited larger tractor with Ferguson System hydraulics was circulated to Massey-Harris-Ferguson dealerships in the form of a publication entitled *Specification and Performance Release SPR 89. Information Vital to your Business. Massey Ferguson MF65 Tractor.* The new MF65 was displayed for the first time to the public at the Smithfield Show in December that year.

Before we look in detail at the specification of this model it would be expedient to consider how it was developed by the Meccano method. The engine chosen was the Perkins P4TA diesel, later called A4.192, driving through an Auburn two-stage clutch to a gearbox that was basically the same as the unit fitted to the MF35. The rear axle could be fitted with a differential lock as optional equipment, and very few early MF65 tractors were sold without one. The rear wheel hubs featured epicyclic reduction gears, which enabled the fitting of larger rear wheels, 11x32 or 13x28, while retaining a top road speed of 14.43mph at 2000rpm.

If we work our way through the specification and layout of the MF65 MkI, its notable features will emerge. The A4.192 engine was a four-cylinder with bore and stroke of 3.5x5in (88.9x127mm) giving a cubic capacity of 192cu.in (3146cc), and a bare-engine output of 50.5bhp at 2000rpm. Being an engine of Perkins design, the cylinder head followed the company's normal practice at the time of an injector nozzle combining a direct and indirect spray pattern, a swirl chamber in the cylinder head and a flat-topped piston. This engine was a developed version of the well-proven P4 but fitted with a CAV distributor-type injector pump.

There was a built-in facility to drive a power steering pump directly off the timing gears. A CAV Thermostart cold-starting aid was fitted to the air intake manifold, which placed a small quantity of diesel in the manifold and then ignited it electrically to warm the incoming air.

The main drive clutch to the gearbox was of

The nearside of the Perkins A4.192 engine. The Ferguson System logo is facing the wrong way.

Cutaway MF65 rear axle illustrates clearly the Goodyear Ausco dry disc brakes and the dog clutch of the differential lock next to the brakes.

POWER STEERING

The '65' can be fitted with full Power Steering. It gives finger-tip steering even with heavy forward loads and reduces operator fatigue on rough land.

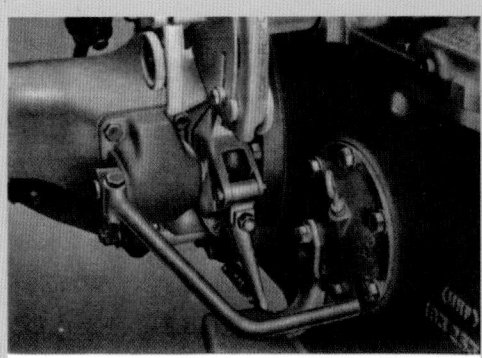

DIFFERENTIAL LOCK

Now a **Standard** fitting. It cancels out the differential on slippery surfaces—gives sure-footed traction to pull you out of wet spots.

LOWER LINKS

Hydraulically operated, these links are fitted with quick-change Cat. 1 and 2 ball-ends as a **Standard** feature. The ends break down to simplify the attachment of heavy implements.

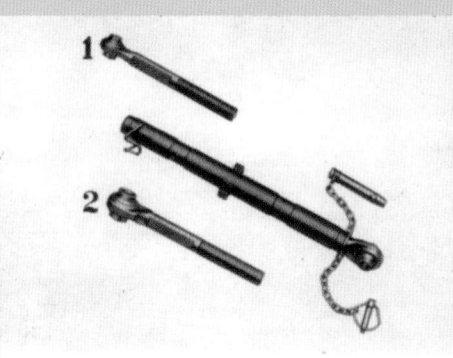

ADJUSTABLE TOP LINK

Category 1 or 2 ball-ends are supplied as **Standard** fittings. The link is adjustable for length. Alternative attachment points on tractor allow accurate work with heavy or light draft implements.

POWERFUL DISC BRAKES

An original **Standard** feature, the disc brakes are sealed against dirt and moisture. Normally used independently, they can be locked together for road work. Automatic compensation for uneven wear.

SWINGING DRAWBAR

Now supplied as a **Standard** fitting the swinging drawbar allows the tractor to turn easily when pulling trailed equipment. It is designed to handle P.T.O. driven equipment with maximum efficiency.

From power steering to swinging drawbar, the MF65 had plenty to offer.

The twin 6 volt
batteries and 11-gallon
(50 litre) fuel tank of
the MF65 MkI.

The detachable ball
ends which lock into
position when the
implement is attached
and the hydraulic
three-point linkage is
raised.

The optional swinging drawbar on the MF65 MkI.

11in (279.4mm) diameter. Pressure was applied by coil springs and released by the first stage of depressing the clutch pedal. The PTO clutch was of 9in (228.6mm) diameter and pressure was applied by a Belleville-type spring (an almost flat open-centred disc of spring steel with a slightly concave profile). The gearbox used more or less the same components as the MF35 gearbox but had higher gear ratios.

The hydraulic system was basically the same as the MF35's. Likewise the option of Multi-Power was offered from August 1962 on the MkII tractors, nearly two years after the MkI had been discontinued and a few months before it was available on the 35X.

The steering system did away with the tradi-

tional Ferguson layout of double drop arms on the steering box, so it became necessary to alter the track rod length if the front wheel track was altered. The steering box was of the worm and peg type, which had very little friction, and the MF65's steering required three-and-a-quarter turns from lock to lock. The arrangement at the front of the tractor hidden behind the radiator grille was as follows: the front end of the drag link was attached to an arm at the top of a vertical shaft that ran through a pedestal housing; the lower end of this shaft had a steering arm attached to it by an indexed spline; this in turn had the inner ends of the track rods attached via conventional track rod ends. The arrangement of the forward part of the steering system allowed the design engineers to incorporate a power steering ram in a fairly straightforward way as an optional extra, able to be fitted at the factory or in the workshop at a later date. This steering arrangement also fitted in very well for tractors made in North America to a tricycle configuration.

The rear brakes, by Girling, were dry discs known as the Ausco type. The design comprised two rotating discs, splined to high-speed half shafts, covered with friction material on both sides. They had an external diameter of 7in (177.8mm) and an internal diameter of 4in (101.6mm), so there was a good area of friction material and they worked efficiently in both directions of rotation. This type of braking system worked well at high speeds, so the faster-running gearbox added to the MF65's braking efficiency. The epicyclic hubs then geared down the rear wheel speed accordingly. The brakes were mounted inboard close to the differential but within their own dry casing, which was provided with a drain hole just in case of leaks!

The two independent brake pedals were located on the right-hand side of the transmission housing adjacent to each other, and could be latched together to provide simultaneous operation. The left pedal was equipped with an over-centre spring-loaded latch; when set and the pedals were depressed to their full travel the pawl engaged with the ratchet quadrant and the brakes were held firmly on. The differential lock was optional and followed the same basic layout as found on the MF35.

The radiator grille was a departure from the slatted designs used previously. It consisted of three panels with a removable centre section made of perforated sheet steel with $\frac{1}{16}$in (1.6mm) diameter staggered holes; the thinking behind this arrangement was that small particles such as chaff, weed seeds and insects collected on the outside could easily be brushed off by hand. Other smaller particles passing through the grille would pass freely through the radiator core fins, which had larger spacings.

The MF65 MkI was fitted with two six-volt batteries linked in series to give 12 volts. As on the MF35, a switch in the starter solenoid circuit ensured that the high-low range lever had to be set in neutral before the starter could be operated. The PTO facilities followed the same format as on the MF35 but it should be noted that a special heavy-duty design of belt pulley assembly was offered as optional equipment; an ingenious quick method of attachment was provided. I have never seen one so I quote, "A single pin passed through the mating parts of a special adaptor and the pulley housing, thus locking the whole assembly to the tractor". The MF35 belt pulley attachment will fit the MF65 but should not be used for high-power applications due, of course, to its lighter design.

The hydraulic system and linkage used on the MF65 MkI were similar to those used on the MF35 but were beefed up to cope with larger and heavier implements. For example, the Scotch yoke four-cylinder pump delivered 57 per cent greater output than that fitted to the TE20 range. The pressure of the system was limited to 2300psi by a safety valve in the pump, which had a flow rate of 3 gallons (13.65 litres) per minute with the engine at 2000rpm. The main hydraulic ram cylinder was bored to 3in (76.225mm), the same as later MF35s (after serial number 65685).

The lift links were materially stronger and slightly longer, with a category II ball connection at the forward end and detachable ball ends at the rear, which enabled a choice to be made between category I or II. Another interesting feature of this lower link was that a spring-loaded latch incorporated towards the outer ends of the hydraulic arm enabled the ball ends to pivot, thereby making attachment of heavy implements easier; this device was the subject of a patent application. One other feature of the lower links was a hole drilled approximately 12in (300mm) from the rear ball ends, which was for use with mid- or rear- mounted implements. The option provided on the MF35 for two alternative attachment points for the lift links was deleted; only one was available. The operation of the MF65's hydraulics was much the same as the MF35's.

Before we conclude this chapter we need to consider the modifications made to the MkI design to turn it into the MkII, whose production began at serial number SNDY 531453 on 9 November 1960. This tractor is still in existence. The main area of change was to the engine, which was now a Perkins AD4.203 direct-injection diesel. This engine had a bore of 3.6in (91.44mm) and a stroke of 5in (127mm), thus increasing the capacity to 203.5cu in (3335cc). With a compression ratio 17.4:1 the power

MASSEY-FERGUSON **65**
MULTI-POWER

a new concept in tractor transmission design

The dash of an MF65R. Note the temperature gauge for the oil in the torque converter transmission. The red arc on the gauge begins at 250°F (120°C) which was considered a maximum; the throttle quadrant is common to the Industrial model.

output at the PTO was 54.9bhp at 2000rpm engine speed. By way of comparison the MkI engine had an output of 46bhp at the PTO, again at 2000rpm – a useful increase. The main external difference between these engines was that the AD4.203 engine had a rectangular one-piece sump whereas the earlier MkI A4.192 engine had a tapered wedge piece bolted into position at the rear of its sump.

Some of the optional equipment offered on the MkI became standard on the MkII, including a differential lock and a full lighting set. A single 12-volt 96AH Lucas battery was fitted in place of the two six-volt batteries on the MkI. This made it possible to increase the capacity of the fuel tank to 14.5 gallons (65.9 litres) when compared to the MkI's capacity of 11 gallons (50 litres).

The option of a high-clearance model was still offered for specialist crop growers, the overall height being 63in (1600mm) compared

Opposite: MF produced this publication in August 1962 when the option of Multi-Power was introduced.

The layout behind the grille of an MF65R Industrial model fitted with power steering.

to the standard height of 58in (1473mm). The standard tractor's ground clearance was 14½in (368mm), while that of this specialist model was 18¾in (476.2mm). This increase was achieved by fitting longer swivel pins to the front axle struts, and at the rear by larger wheels, with 11x38 or 12x38 tyres. The attachment points for the lower links to maintain the standard height of 20in (508mm) from ground level was achieved by the fitting of special fabricated brackets bolted to each side of the rear axle housing.

To round off this chapter on the MF65 it is important to look at the industrial versions that were available with the introduction of the MF65 MkII. Letter suffixes were used to differentiate between models fitted with the standard clutch and gearbox, designated MF65S, while those fitted with instant reverse transmission and torque convertor drive were designated MF65R.

The most noticeable feature that set both models apart from the Agricultural tractors was the use of Massey Ferguson Industrial Yellow for the wheels and sheet metalwork. The braking arrangements necessary to comply with the Road Traffic Act required these tractors to have two independent braking systems in place. This was achieved by retaining the normal inboard dry disc brakes, operated by a pair of foot pedals placed on the right-hand side of the transmission, which could be used independently or latched together for highway use. The second system was provided for

Bob Parker's MF65 High Clearance, showing the extended front axle legs and king pins. This model was mostly used for row crop work.

The MF65 High Clearance has 38-inch rear wheels, while the fronts are the standard 16-inch.

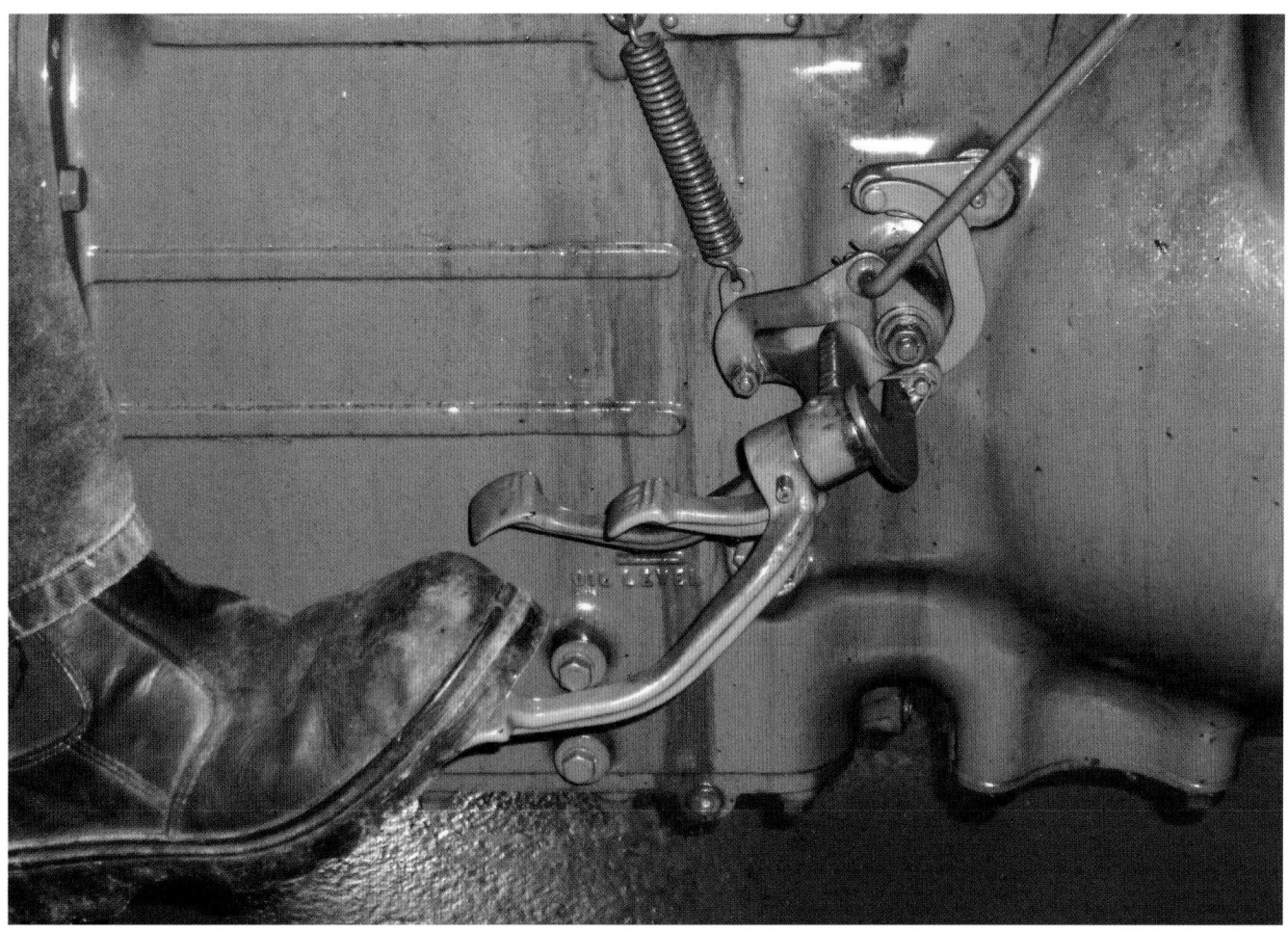

parking purposes and was operated by a hand-brake lever on the left connected via a linkage to 14x2in drum brakes - more or less similar to those fitted on the TE20 tractor - attached to the rear wheel hubs. A smaller modification was the fitment of a toothed quadrant, just below the hand throttle lever on the dash panel, to ensure that the selected throttle setting was retained. A horn and mirror were fitted to tractors equipped with dual brakes, again to meet legal requirements.

The design of the front axle differed from that of Agricultural models in that it was made of heavier steel sections and was not adjustable; power steering was standard. As optional equipment a hydraulic pump could be mounted at the front of the tractor just below the radiator, taking its drive directly off the front end of the crankshaft through a coupling. This would be used to power a heavy-duty front loader or back actor equipment.

The layout of the instant reverse and torque converter drive system needs to be considered in some detail. For industrial work these tractors were generally fitted with front-end loaders where rapid and frequent changes of direction were required. Drive from the flywheel was taken through a torque converter, the output shaft of which connected to a set of constant-mesh primary reduction gears; power was then taken through a selectable set of two-speed sliding spur gears controlled by the main gear lever. This was compounded by a planetary reduction gear set on the output end of the main shaft, controlled by the smaller gear lever.

To create the instant reverse facility two multi-plate clutches were combined with a reverse gear train; engagement of the forward clutch locked the input shaft to the output shaft whilst engagement of the reverse clutch caused drive to go through the lay shaft and reverse idler gear, thereby reversing the rotation of the output shaft. This feature was controlled by a set of three small clutch pedals on the right-hand

The direction and speed control pedals on the MF65R, with the driver's foot here operating in forward mode.

The engine of the MKII MF65 and its features explained.

This is the new 4-A-203D engine — the heart of the MORE POWERFUL '65' tractor. It's a four-cylinder diesel unit, with direct injection for fuel economy and quick starting. It develops a full 13% more power than the earlier model, PLUS 16½% more torque! This gives even greater lugging power—and to keep the engine "hanging on" to the load, maximum torque is developed at only 1200 r.p.m. So the '65' will carry you through the toughest spots in the field without faltering.

Yet despite this extra power, fuel consumption is low. Advanced design features in the engine give you increased output at lower cost than ever before!

Cylinder liners are chromium plated to reduce wear, ensure long life and cut down oil consumption. The sensitive mechanical governor opens up in a flash. The fuel tank capacity has been increased to 14½ gallons. This, together with increased engine economy gives you longer running periods without stops to refuel. A single 12-volt battery reduces replacement costs.

And as a final extra — a special COLD-START MODEL is available for use in areas where temperatures are extremely low.

side of the transmission casing, the brake pedals being moved to the left-hand side; these clutch pedals also acted as foot throttles controlling engine speed once the clutch had engaged. A third and centrally-placed pedal controlled just engine speed when neither clutch was engaged. The outer clutch pedal gave forward drive while the inner pedal provided reverse. It should be noted that on tractors with this type of transmission the PTO shaft would turn anticlockwise when the reverse pedal was depressed - a useful feature when operating a linkage-mounted post-hole digger in rooty or stony ground! These tractors could not be tow-started.

One final small but important feature of these tractors was the provision for a dash-mounted transmission oil temperature gauge; overheating could be caused by operating in too high a gear, which could obviously cause serious damage. The likelihood of overheating was reduced by fitting a cooler in the oil circuit, placed in front of the radiator core but behind the grille. This type of transmission operated most reliably under the arduous conditions in which these tractors generally worked and was later widely adopted on other Massey Ferguson industrial equipment.

The tyre sizes were quoted as 7.50x16 (either six- or eight-ply) on the front wheels, the rears being 14x28 six-ply. On these tyre sizes the MF65R gave a maximum road speed of 19mph (30.6kph) in fourth gear at the rated engine speed of 2000rpm – quite fast for its day!

So with production of the MF65 starting on Tuesday 11 March 1958 at serial number 500001 and ending in the early part of winter 1964 (apologies for being vague but records are sadly not quite complete) at 614024 it means a total of 11,4023 units were produced over approximately five-and-a-half years; this was, of course, alongside the production of MF35s. This model range gave way to the 100 series or Red Giants (ie the MF130, MF135, MF165 and MF175) launched at the Smithfield show in December 1964.

Right: A rather moth-eaten front cover of an early MF65 publication promoting the MF65 Mk II.

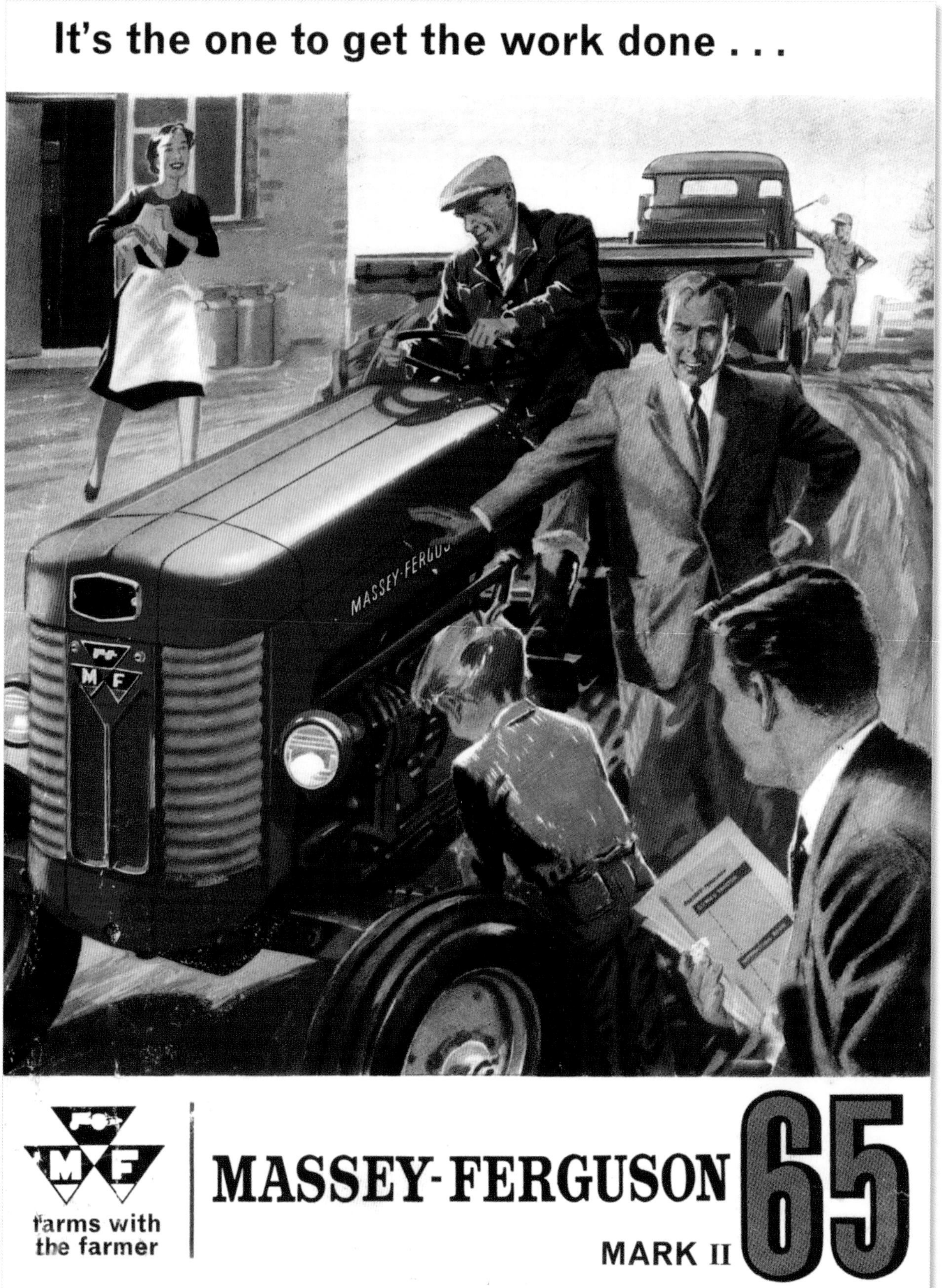

It's the one to get the work done . . .

farms with the farmer

MASSEY-FERGUSON 65
MARK II

Chapter Five

Implements

A vast range of implements had been available to the user of the Ferguson TE20. With the advent of its successor the FE35, and later the MF35, MF35X and MF65, new implement designs were put in hand and existing designs were beefed up. The FE35 was manufactured from September 1956, and continued as the MF35 and then MF35X until production ceased in late 1964. Meanwhile, production of the MF65 MkI started in 1958 and ran on until late 1964, albeit as the MF65 MkII.

With such a lengthy production span, two quite different sizes of tractors and the resulting choice of implements, it's possible that this chapter may contain some errors and omissions. Equipment that was clearly of Massey-Harris design is not included.

With TE20 production coming to a close, to be replaced by a more developed and more powerful FE35, Massey-Harris-Ferguson product engineers had to develop a range of implements that took full advantage of the improved specifications, which offered increased horsepower and the extra feature of position control available on the hydraulic system, along with the enlarged diameter of the PTO shaft (1⅜in diameter with six splines) that brought it in line with SAE standards.

To help users who operated both TE20 and FE35 tractors, a most concise and informative manual was produced in May 1956, *Implement and Accessory Adaptation*, running to 57 pages. This booklet listed Ferguson implements that could be attached to the FE35 without modification, plus implements and accessories that could only be used with TE20 tractors.

As this is a lengthy chapter it seems prudent to divide the implements into sections under the general headings found in Massey Ferguson's December 1962 *Facts and Figures* sales guide

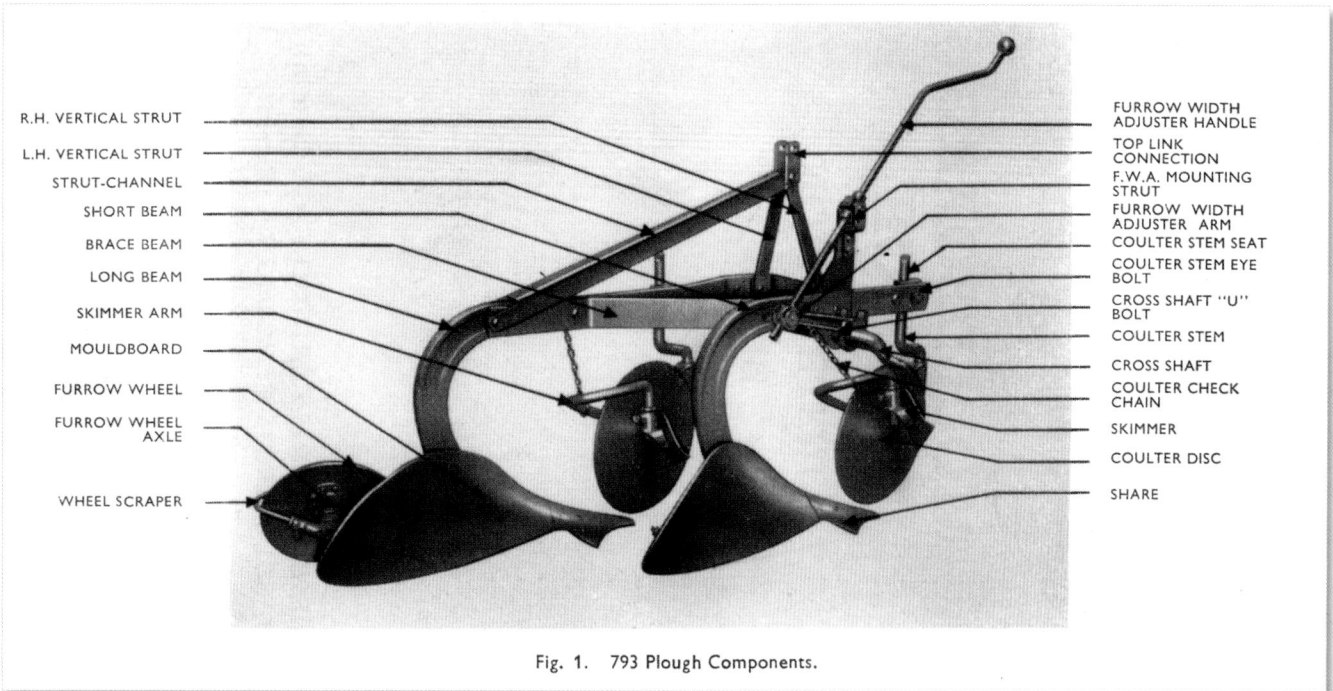

R.H. VERTICAL STRUT
L.H. VERTICAL STRUT
STRUT-CHANNEL
SHORT BEAM
BRACE BEAM
LONG BEAM
SKIMMER ARM
MOULDBOARD
FURROW WHEEL
FURROW WHEEL AXLE
WHEEL SCRAPER

FURROW WIDTH ADJUSTER HANDLE
TOP LINK CONNECTION
F.W.A. MOUNTING STRUT
FURROW WIDTH ADJUSTER ARM
COULTER STEM SEAT
COULTER STEM EYE BOLT
CROSS SHAFT "U" BOLT
COULTER STEM
CROSS SHAFT
COULTER CHECK CHAIN
SKIMMER
COULTER DISC
SHARE

Fig. 1. 793 Plough Components.

issued to dealers' sales representatives. The format was as follows: Tillage, Planting, Fertilizing, Hay & Forage, and Miscellaneous.

Tillage

Let us delve into the tillage implements developed for the FE35/MF65 tractor. The basic plough range was known as the 793 and had clear lineage from the TE20 era. Most of these ploughs were available with a wide range of bases or bodies, which could in turn be fitted with a variety of shares. The bases were given letter designations, and what follows gives the code letter and then a brief description of type:

The **L** base or body was good for autumn ploughing of heavy stubble. It worked satisfactorily to a depth of 9in (228.6mm).

H base was considered a general-purpose type, leaving a well set-up furrow slice suitable for depths of about 8in (203mm).

B base was a semi-digger type with good burying characteristics and a broken furrow slice; it worked satisfactorily to about 9in (228mm).

N base was a digger type with the share cutting almost the whole width of the furrow slice,

again displaying good burying qualities. It operated to 12in (300mm).

C base was a deep digger type featuring a relatively short mouldboard with a strong concave profile and operated to a depth of 14in (356mm).

Y and **U** type bases used a bar point.

W type bases or bodies had a two-piece share and a replaceable mouldboard shin, and worked to a depth of 10in (254mm). Their characteristics were halfway between general purpose and semi-digger, with good ability to bury trash and hence a neat finish to ploughing. The profile of the body followed that of the N type.

The 793 range was available in the following configurations: the 10in (254mm) frame was produced in two-, three-, four- and five-furrow widths, and fitted with either H or B bases, or as an alternative, still with 10in (254mm) frame, could be fitted with L and W bases but only in two-, three- or four-furrow configurations. The 12in (305mm) frame could be made up into two-, three- or four-furrow widths and could be fitted with B, N, L, Y or W bases. The 14in (356mm) frame was only produced in two- and three-furrow sizes and could be fitted

From the 1958 MF instruction book on the 793 range of mouldboard ploughs; note the single arm disc coulter.

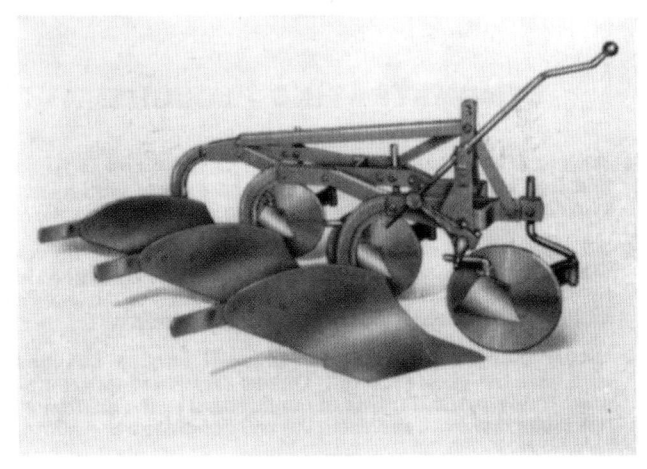

798 PLOUGH

Dimensions (3-furrow)

Overall Length	. . 107″
Overall width	. . 56″
Overall height	. . 41½″.
Total weight	. . 872 lb.

Bases Available

16″ frame	. . 1, 2 and 3 furrow 'C', 'N' and 'Y' bases.

SPECIAL FEATURES

★ The 798 Plough is designed for 16″ furrow width ploughing down to a depth of 14″.

★ It is available with either 'C', 16″ 'N' or 16″ 'Y' type bases which are similar to the bases used on the 793 Ploughs but slightly deeper in the mouldboard to match the wider share used to obtain a 16″ furrow width. The brace beams are 3″ × 1″ in section to meet the demands imposed on the modern plough by greater tractor power and faster speeds.

★ The curved 'hook' beams supporting the bases are specially strengthened to withstand shock loadings.

★ Excellent trash clearing properties are ensured by the horizontal spacing of 25″ provided between each base. This together with a vertical clearance of approx. 23¾″ between the share and the underside of the beam, means easy working in heavy top growth.

★ Single or double arm coulters of 18″ diameter are available. Single arm coulters allow the skimmers to be positioned for better burying of stubble as well as undercutting the furrow wall to produce crested furrow slices. These furrow slices give better drainage allowing water to run away quickly to the furrow bottom.

These details of the MF798 plough are taken from a 1962 MF salesman's manual.

with either N or Y bases.

To complete the specification of the 793 range of ploughs it should be noted that they could be specified with either single- or double-arm coulters. The double-arm type had the advantage of a bearing each side of the disc, and was produced with a fixed undercut of 3in;

in contrast, single-arm coulters were adjustable over a slightly wider range of angles. The discs themselves were of 15½in (394mm) diameter and made of heat-treated high-carbon steel. The skimmer blades were made of a similar material and were 9in (228mm). There was a beam-to-share clearance of 22in (558mm). The furrow wheel was spring-loaded and of 13in (330mm) diameter, flexibly mounted on the rear landside; this wheel was fitted with an adjustable scraper. A single-furrow plough was also produced in this series, equipped with a deep digger base, an 18in (457mm) disc and a 12in (304mm) skimmer. All in all, it was a popular and wide-selling range of ploughs, but perhaps I am biased because I use one.

The next plough in the Massey Ferguson line-up for us to consider was the 794, which was a bar point design. It is worth elaborating on the advantages of bar point, as well as a brief look at its specification. The main advantage is that is almost impossible to break a bar point, being made of solid rectangular carbon steel to EN45 specification. Set at a pitch angle of 12-degrees, the bar was 16in (406mm) long, notched at 1in (25.4mm) intervals to aid adjustment and location. The bar was positioned on the outside of the base for easy adjustment. The frame was made in only a 12in (305mm) width and in only two- or three-furrow configurations, and had to be fitted with Y or U bases. The disc diameter was the same as the 793 plough's, and conventional skimmers could be added. Alternatively, Scotch skimmers could be specified, making the plough a bit lighter.

The general construction of these ploughs was slightly heavier than the 793 range, and the beam-to-share clearance of 25in (635mm) was slightly greater. A front furrow width adjuster within easy reach of the ploughman was fitted as standard. A 16in (406mm) single-furrow plough was also produced in this range, fitted with deep digger body and an 18in (457mm) disc with 12in (304mm) skimmer.

Moving on to the last of the conventional ploughs offered to users in this period we come to the 798 range, which was intended to be coupled to the MF65 tractor. The three-furrow version weighed in at 872lb (396kg). This type was produced in one-, two- and three-furrow versions with a set frame width of 16in (406mm,) and could operate down to a depth of 14in (353mm). C, N and Y bases could be specified, with single- or double-arm coulters to carry the 18in (457mm) diameter discs. It was a heavy-duty plough for a larger farmer or contractor.

Turning now to the range of reversible ploughs marketed by Massey Ferguson in the period covered by this book, the 796 was a 16in (406mm) single-furrow model, virtually the same as the plough marketed in the TE20 era as the T-AE-28 and therefore covered in the book *Ferguson TE20 In Detail*.

The 797 Two-Furrow Reversible Plough had a novel turn-over mechanism whereby the whole plough frame was turned through 180 degrees by an external hydraulic circuit; this function was achieved thus: within the centre part of the plough's cross shaft (cast integrally with the whole headstock) there was a toothed rack activated from each end by independent small hydraulic rams, again built into the cast headstock. The mainframe of the plough was mounted on a substantial bearing integral with the headstock. A toothed pinion fixed to the body of the plough engaged with the toothed rack so that when hydraulic pressure was applied to one ram the rack moved, thus turning the main frame through 180 degrees. Applying

oil pressure to the other ram caused the plough frame to rotate in the opposite direction. It is believed that this design was of French origin.

These ploughs were made in three formats: a 10in (254mm) frame that could be equipped with H or L bases; a 12in (304mm) frame that could be fitted with N, Y or L bases; or a 14in

A prototype two-furrow reversible plough, fitted to a French-registered tractor, and a close-up of the hydraulic head.

This 1961 cutaway drawing of the head stock of the MF797 two-furrow reversible plough clearly shows its inner workings.

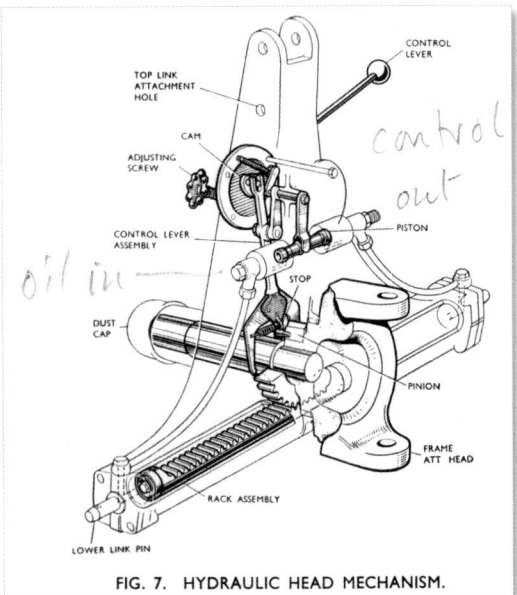

FIG. 7. HYDRAULIC HEAD MECHANISM.

A nice period close-up of the MF85-7 three-furrow reversible plough at work. Note the safety roller catch built into each of the six beams. Dated December 1962.

(356mm), which could only be equipped with N or Y bases. The front furrow width was set by adjuster screws on the frame head. Either single- or double-arm coulters were available and could be fitted with skimmers.

The final plough to be described in this section was designated 85-7, made only suitable for category II linkage and generally sold as a three-furrow unit. The frames could be arranged to give either 12in (306mm) or 14in (356mm), and they weighed in at approximately 1500lb (623 kg). The disc coulters were 15½in (393.7mm) and were available mounted on either single- or double-arm brackets. It should be mentioned that each individual base was adjustable for pitch, but all needed to be set the same so that the plough performed properly. A special safety feature of the 85-7 was that built into the base support beam was a spring-loaded roller catch that released the beam to pivot rearwards if the base struck an obstruction; the degree of tension was adjustable. To reset, the driver just had to reverse slightly once clear of the obstruction. The turnover mechanism built into the headstock was entirely self-energising: on lifting, the plough would automatically turn through 180 degrees.

The heavy weight of this plough (1380-1550lb, 627-704kg) meant it was necessary to use a full complement of weights placed on the

It's easy to get a good seedbed with M-F Discs!

The 8' model

DISC ANGLING

Quick—positive—no juggling! Separate levers for front and rear gangs let you vary disc angles to keep a level tilth. All done from the tractor seat.

SPECIFICATION

front weight frame. The advantage of one-way ploughing was that it needed no marking out or finishing; it needed only a shallow single furrow spaced out from the boundary by about six yards (5.48m); Massey Ferguson recommended it should be turned towards the land being ploughed. Once the headland had been marked out, ploughing could commence in a straightforward way. The precision of finishing was done away with, so relatively unskilled drivers could produce good work and save time.

Turning now to the implements that would follow ploughing in seed bed preparation, the smallest and lightest in the range of disc harrows offered by Massey Ferguson was the 765 Offset Disc Harrow, which had a working width of just 5ft 3in (1600mm) but could be extended to a maximum of 7ft 3in (2210mm), and was more or less identical to the harrows produced for use with the TE20 tractor. The

765's ability to be offset by 2ft (609mm) to either side made it ideally suited to orchard work; 20in (508mm) diameter discs were fitted, spaced at 9in (229mm) intervals, and with shafts carried on white iron bearings of dust-excluding design, the implement weighed about 812lb (369kg).

The 722 Mounted Disc Harrow was again similar to the type produced for the TE20 (designated 2A-BE-22) but was made available in three widths: 6ft (1829mm), 7ft (2134mm) and 8ft (2438mm), fitted with 20, 24 or 28 plain or scalloped discs of 18in (457mm) diameter. The bearings were oil-impregnated hardwood. The front and rear gangs could be adjusted independently by two levers each with five settings, giving a pitch range from parallel to 20 degrees. The 6ft (1829mm) harrow was fitted only with category I attachment pins but other sizes were equipped with both category I and II pins that could be bolted to the frame at slightly different

The MF722 Mounted Disc Harrow, from an MF sales brochure dated June 1962.

The MF749 Mounted Disc Harrow, coupled to an MF65 tractor. Note the weights in the frame of the harrow.

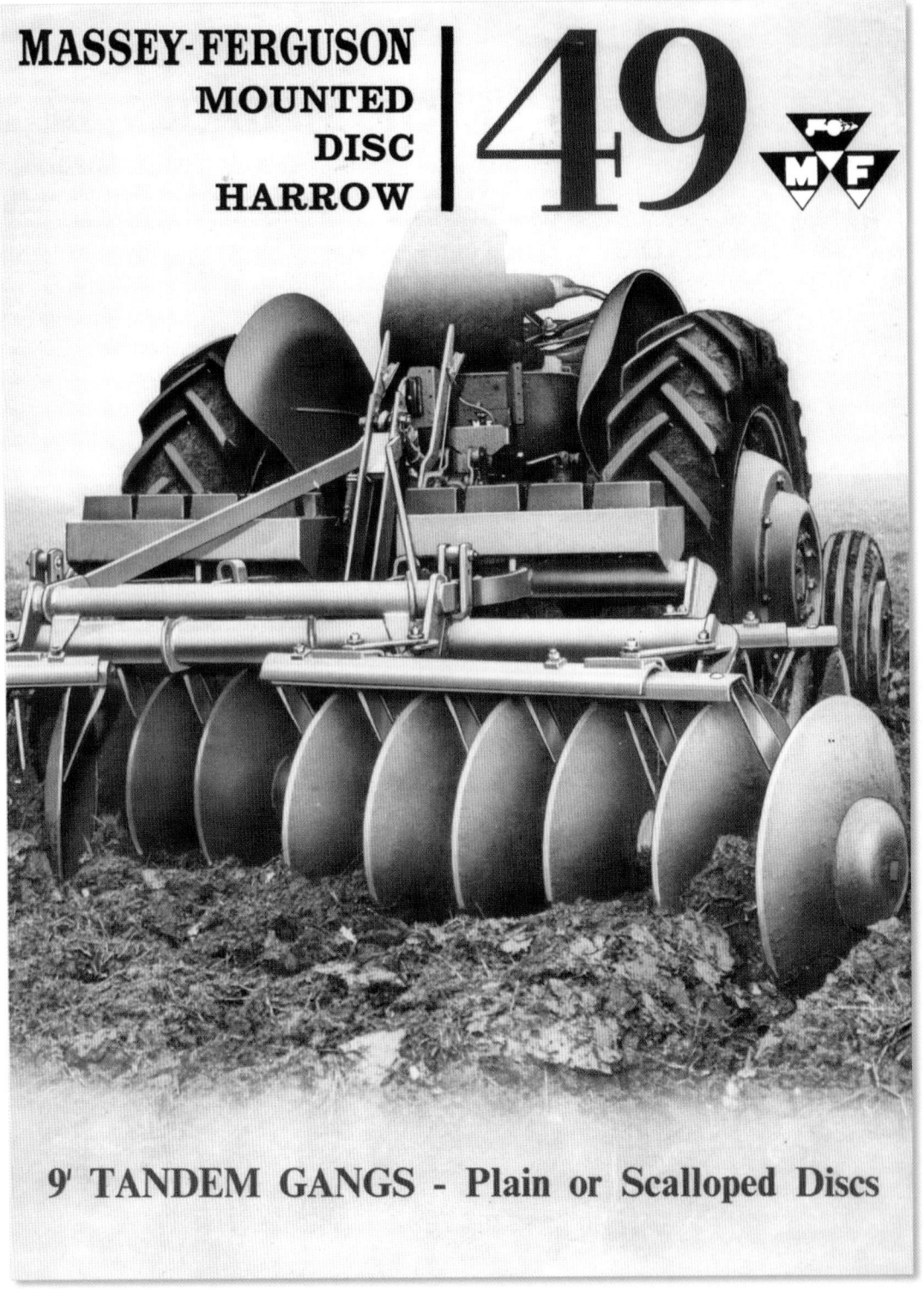

MASSEY-FERGUSON MOUNTED DISC HARROW **49** MF

9' TANDEM GANGS - Plain or Scalloped Discs

heights – the higher position gave greater sensitivity to the tractor's draft control system, while the lower position gave greater clearance for transporting the harrow. The disc scrapers were adjustable, and the 8ft (2438mm) model weighed 840lb (382kg).

The heaviest disc harrow on offer was the 749, which had an operating width of 9ft (2743mm) and weighed 1512lb (687kg), obviously designed to team up with the MF65 tractor

MASSEY-FERGUSON
49 MOUNTED DISC HARROW

Specification

MOUNTING

Category 1 and 2; three-point linkage.

FRAME

Heavy duty, welded tubular construction. Two built-in weight trays with space for 8×56 lb. weights.

DISC GANGS

Four gangs each comprising six discs, spindle, spacer spools, bearing assemblies and scraper supports. Gang assembly clamped up together by Philidas lock nuts on spindle ends. Discs at 8″ spacing.

DISC GANG ANGLING

Independent levers and linkage to front and rear pairs of gangs.

GANG BEARINGS

Triple-sealed, self-aligning, pre-packed ball bearings.

DISCS

Optional plain or scalloped type. Either 22″ or 24″ diameter.

DIMENSIONS AND WEIGHT

(*Dimensions with gangs angled at 20° and 24″ scalloped discs fitted*).

Overall length	...	...	...	5′ 11″
Overall height	...	...	...	4′ 8½″
Length from lower link pins	...	...	5′ 8″
Height to Cat. 2 top link hole	...	...	3′ 9½″
Overall width	...	...	...	9′ 2½″
Weight (approx.)	...	...	...	1500 lbs.

Set a date—we'll demonstrate

J.B. Printed in England.

Massey-Ferguson reserve the right to change specifications and improve machines without obligation regarding machines purchased before or after such changes are made.

UKMF 331/26L/30

although it had linkage facilities for category I and II. The discs fitted to this model could be 22in (559mm) or 24in (610mm), either plain or scalloped; there were 24 in total, arranged in two individually adjustable gangs between parallel and 20 degrees. They were controlled by a pair of levers within reach of the driver. A front weight frame was fitted as standard. Eight self-aligning pre-packed bearings were fitted, each embracing triple seals.

for efficient rowcrop aeration and weed control....

Thorough Cultivation between rows - - - at any width !

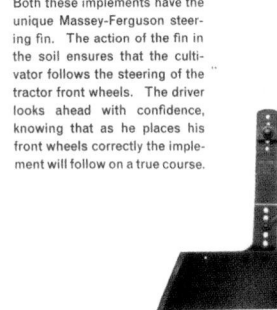

The Steerage Fin

Both these implements have the unique Massey-Ferguson steering fin. The action of the fin in the soil ensures that the cultivator follows the steering of the tractor front wheels. The driver looks ahead with confidence, knowing that as he places his front wheels correctly the implement will follow on a true course.

Turning now to tine-type tillers, the 738 was manufactured in 9-, 11- and 13-tine versions with working widths of 80in (2032mm), 98in (2489mm) or 120in (3048mm), and with weights of 290lb (131.8kg), 530lb (241kg) and 590lb (260.1kg) respectively. To ensure a robust construction the main frame was made of high-carbon steel angle with fixing holes at 1in (25.4mm) cross centres to enable tine spacing to be set as required. The two larger models had additional tubular bracing to resist torsional loads; the tines were arranged fore and aft in two staggered rows.

An interesting and practical feature of this range of tillers was that each tine had its own spring-controlled break-back mechanism to protect the individual tines should they strike an obstruction. A range of reversible points was marketed to widen the versatility of the tiller. These included shovel points, which were produced in two sizes – 2in (50mm) or 2½in (63mm) wide. The duck foot sweeps were either 6in (150mm) or 8in (200mm), and were non-reversible. The grassland or Alfa teeth were reversible.

The 721 Rigid Tine Cultivator was a light-

The rigid tine 721 (top) and spring tine 720 (bottom) cultivators.

A nice 1961 shot of the MF736 29-tine Flexi-Harrow making full use of the MF65 Mk1's 50hp. Note the skids placed in the stowed position, allowing a good depth of soil penetration.

weight implement intended for row-crop cultivation. Its design closely followed the Ferguson 9-KE-20. The nine rigid tines mounted in two rows to a high-carbon steel angle frame with holes drilled at 1in (25mm) cross centres, which allowed a wide range of settings. Like all Massey Ferguson row-crop cultivators it was fitted with a steerage fin to help ensure that it followed the steering of the tractor's front wheels. This model was made in one width only, that being 84in (2100mm) and with a weight of 274lb (124.5kg).

Also equipped with a steerage fin was the 720 Spring Tine Cultivator, which was 86in (2184mm) wide; it closely followed the Ferguson-95-KE-20 model in its design. Nine forged heat-treated high-carbon steel stems of 1¼in (31.75mm) bolted to the main frame of this implement, which was identical to the previous model. Nine tines made of curved and concentric sprung steel 1¾in (44.5mm) wide were bolted to the stems. The juncture between the stems and tine provided a horizontal adjustment facility of 4in (101mm).

Like the rigid tine cultivator, the same alternative types and sizes of replaceable tine points could be fitted.

The MF736 Flexi-Harrow was an interesting implement introduced to the range in March 1961 and was marketed in two model sizes - a 21-tine version had a working width of 6ft (2032mm), whilst the 29-tine model had a working width of 9ft 4in (2845mm); both were fitted with category I and II linkage pins, and either depth wheels or skids were available. With a land wheel either side, the 21-tine machine weighed 414lb (187.8kg), while the 29-tine cultivator with wheels weighed 564lb (225.8kg). Both sizes could be fully- or loose-mounted. For accurate depth control at less than 4in (101mm) it was recommended that land wheels or skids were used. The Massey Ferguson instruction manual suggested that the Flexiharrow should be operated as fast as ground conditions allowed (or how tough the tractor driver was!).

Carried over from the Ferguson TE20 era was the MF709 Weeder, which had a working width of 155in (3930mm) but by folding the outer end sections into the transport position the width was reduced to 116in (2940mm). It featured 71 high-carbon spring steel teeth with pointed and round ends, which were adjustable along the

Part of a 1960 leaflet for the MF709 Weeder.

**Weed up to 50 acres in One day
High Speed . . . Low Cost . . . Effective Control**

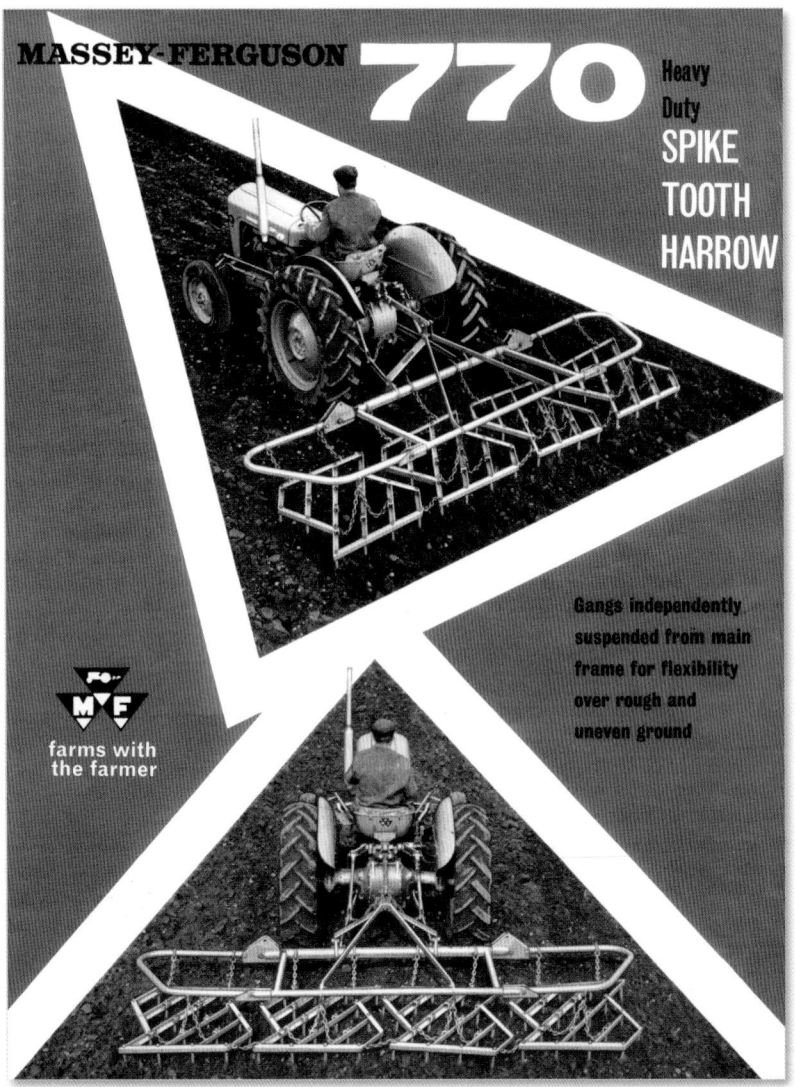

MASSEY-FERGUSON **770** Heavy Duty **SPIKE TOOTH HARROW**

MF farms with the farmer

Gangs independently suspended from main frame for flexibility over rough and uneven ground

The MF727 Subsoiler fitted with pipe laying attachment.

What better way is there of illustrating this MF770 Heavy Duty Harrow?

front and rear of its light-but-strong steel angle frame. In general use it would be set to give complete ground coverage but for row-crop work the tines could be moved or taken off altogether as required. Again a high operating speed was used to achieve a rate of up to 50 acres (20.24 hectares) per day; it was most effective when weeds were small, at the four-leaf stage, and with dry soil conditions.

The MF770 Heavy Duty Harrow was a significantly stronger version of the Ferguson S-BE-31 harrow. This implement had a heavy-duty tubular main frame with end sections that could be folded for transportation; it was equipped with both category I and II linkage pins. Each of the four zigzag harrow frames was suspended from the main frame and from the folding sections by chains, and each section was linked

to its neighbour, again by chains. This harrow was particularly effective working rough undulating ground. Its working width was 12ft 9in (3886mm) and in transport mode 8ft 6½in (2603.5mm). It weighed 500lb (227kg).

The Massey Ferguson 727 Subsoiler was a complete departure from the earlier Ferguson model D-BE-28 in that it was of a much more robust construction but weighed less than half that of the Ferguson model. The cross shaft for attachment to the tractor's lower link was a standard Ferguson nine-hole drawbar, and therefore to category I dimensions. The frame was bolted to that. The main beam was of high-carbon steel terminating in a replaceable double-ended hardened and tempered share; it operated to a maximum depth of 21in (233mm). To increase the versatility of this subsoiler a pipe- or cable-laying attachment could be added, able to bury pipes of 1½in (38mm) diameter to a depth of 16in (406mm). It was claimed to be capable of operation up to 3.5mph, obviously very dependent on ground conditions; the use of stabilisers was not recommended. No support stand was provided to ensure it remained upright when parked off the tractor.

Planting

Various planters and seeders were marketed during the period covered by this book, so let us first look at the MF32 Unit Seeder manufactured by Russell's (Kirbymoorside) Ltd, Yorkshire. The frame had a width of 9ft 5in (2870mm) and the six-seeder, land wheel-driven model weighed 656lb (298kg); PTO-driven models were heavier. As each individual seeder unit was an expensive item in its own right, Massey Ferguson offered the choice of four, five or six units fitted to a machine. Obviously, if one purchased the full six, units could be taken off as required. The purpose of this (advanced for its time) seeder was to produce precision sowing for a wide range of seed sizes and to be able to alter spacing, thus economising on seed and subsequent thinning.

As an alternative to the land drive model just outlined, a PTO version was produced to overcome any tendency for the land drive wheels to slip under adverse ground conditions. Drive from the tractor's PTO was taken via the usual jointed shaft to a covered chain and four-sprocket drive set. These sprockets could be interchanged to provide different ratios between PTO and cell wheel speed. For operation with Massey Ferguson tractors equipped with ground speed PTO it was suggested that this mode should be used. The PTO shaft drove the lower sprocket, with power transmitted by a roller chain to a top sprocket, either side of which were placed, on the left-hand side an idler sprocket and on the right-hand side a sprocket adjustable to provide chain tensioning. The top sprocket drove the input shaft of a small 90-degree bevel gearbox, on the output side of which was a peg clutch operated by a lever with a short chain attached..The other end of the chain was anchored to a small bracket bolted to the right-hand lower link; this was to ensure that when the seeder was lifted by the three-point linkage the cell wheels ceased to rotate. Drive was transmitted from the peg clutch by roller chain to the main cross shaft, incorporating a full-length keyway supported on four sealed bearings and located below the tool bar. Seven vee-pulleys (six of which were adjustable, the seventh being fixed at the centre line of the machine and could be used as a datum point) could be selected to provide take-off points for the primary belt drive to the seeder units.

This belt was provided with a spring-loaded tension pulley that compensated for variation in linkage geometry due to vertical articulation caused by land undulations. A twin vee-pulley mounted on the seeder's individual frame picked up this drive; the adjacent vee drove the secondary belt, which transmitted rotational movement to a roller chain and sprocket mounted within a case on the outside of the seed hopper. This arrangement enabled the cell wheel to turn slower than the repeller wheel. A more basic two-row roller model was produced, targeted towards the smaller farmer who chose to grow root crops on ridges.

As optional equipment an electrically-operated system which monitored seeding action could be fitted to this unit seeder. It featured an indicator light panel fitted to the dashboard of the tractor within view of the driver, which comprised an on-off switch (taking its supply

Massey-Ferguson

No. 32
UNIT
SEEDER

Accurate single seed spacing for easier thinning and cultivation of row crops

Massey-Ferguson farms with the farmer

A working view of the MF32 Unit Seeder. Note the P.A.V.T rear wheels fitted to the MF35.

A more basic two-row roller model of the Unit Seeder.

from the tractor's electrics) plus six indicator lights – five red and one green. Other components were fitted to each individual seeder unit and consisted of a micro-switch adjacent to each cell wheel, arranged so that the contacts opened and closed as the wheel rotated, which in turn caused the five red lights to

The Unit Seeder's sprocket drive arrangement, variable to suit the type of tractor in use.

An MF publicity shot of an MF35 with a potato harvester. Both tractors are fitted with PAVT rear wheels

flash; the lights indicated the status of units one to five. Number six hopper was wired to the green indicator light and would flash in the same manner as the others. Number six hopper had, in addition to the cell wheel switch, a float switch to monitor seed level in this hopper, which would light continuously when the seed level fell dangerously low. It was important to fill this hopper with slightly less seed than the others in order to retain this warning facility.

The MF726 Potato Planter was basically the same as the Ferguson P-PE-B20, which in reality was a kit of parts fitted to the Ferguson three-row ridger R-DE-20 and required three people to operate it; the tractor driver and two operators each sat on a pan seat facing inwards towards a central potato hopper, which had a capacity of 392lb (178kg). Spacing was controlled by a bell signal device that prompted each operator to drop a potato down the feed chute of his or her row. The bell striker in turn was driven by cams formed on the disc within the rim of the land-driven wheel; these cams were arranged in four concentric circles thus giving spacing of 8in (203mm), 10in (254mm), 12in (305mm), 16in (406mm) or, with an extension rim fitted, up to 20in (305mm). To extend the range of planting even further it was suggested that operators could drop a potato every other bell ping – an idea that sounded as if it might produce some odd spacing!

The MF718 Automatic Potato Planter clearly illustrates the machine's layout. Front wheel weights were necessary to maintain steerability when the planter was fully loaded and raised clear of the ground.

A fertilizer attachment was produced for this planter, chain-driven from a sprocket bolted to the centre of the left-hand rear wheel. Ten different application rates could be set by selecting two out of the five sprockets supplied with the kit. Fertilizer was placed in bands away from the tubers. The hopper of this attachment held 190lb (86.3kg) of material and had application rates of 616lb (208kg) to 3192lb (1451kg) per acre; a reduced delivery kit was also marketed.

Another major advance in the bid to reduce labour requirement was the development and introduction of the MF718 Automatic Potato Planter, which required only the tractor driver to operate it, whereas the previous model (described above) needed three people. These planters were land wheel-driven, had two hoppers mounted on the framework and were attached to the tractor's linkage using either

The 726 Potato Planter and Fertilizer Attachment. Dated February 1960

The MF732 Multi-Purpose Seed Drill. It was claimed that apart from sowing cereals this machine could virtually handle all the range of seeds likely to be found in farming and vegetable growing businesses. Note the extended front wheel track, further increased by reversing the wheel centres.

category I or II pins; needless to say they incorporated a steerage fin. The ridge shape was formed by discs. The combined capacity of the two hoppers was 672lb (305kg), and the width between the rows was adjustable so settings of 24in (610mm), 26in (660mm), 28in (711mm) and 30in (762 mm) could be obtained. Likewise, the seed potato space could be set to give the following options: 10in (245mm), 12in (305mm), 16in (406mm) or 18in (457mm) depending on the choice of drive sprockets. As optional equipment a 22-tooth sprocket was offered, giving a potato spacing of 8in (203mm), which was ideal

for planting potatoes grown for seed. When using the automatic planter it was essential to use graded seed. The depth of planting was controlled by a three-position share on each feed chute. This machine had a dry weight of 875lb (397.7kg). A fertilizer attachment was produced to mate with this planter; it was along the same lines as that fitted to the MF726 model, but the hopper was extended to hold 336lb (152.7kg) of fertilizer.

The MF372 multi-purpose drill and fertilizer attachment was, in lots of ways, a development of the Ferguson universal seed drill with fertilizer attachment and is described in the book *Ferguson TE20 In Detail*. It was a semi-mounted trailed machine with 13 rows, the seed hopper having a capacity of 7.7cu.ft (22cu.m), while the fertilizer hopper held approx 336lb (approx 152kg). A wider 15-row model was also marketed, with slightly increased capacities. A category I linkage was only offered on these drills, while the tyre size was 6.50x16.

The MF728 Grain and Fertilizer Drill was really a Massey-Harris machine made in 13-, 15- and 20-row versions, trailed and mounted on steel wheels – not ideal for transportation on the highway!

The MF721 Trailed Spinner Broadcaster.

Fertilizing

In the area of plain fertilizing implements, the MF717 Fertilizer Distributor was a direct derivative of a Massey-Harris machine, being trailed and running on steel wheels. A choice of widths was offered: a seven-plate machine had an overall width of 9ft (2743mm) or an eight-plate version was 10ft (3048mm).

The MF721 Trailed Spinner Broadcaster was mounted on a pair of 4.00x12 traction-type tyres to provide drive through a 90-degree gearbox to a spinning disc and a concentric contra-rotating agitator. The drive from the land wheels could be disengaged for transportation.

The other spinner broadcaster, the MF22-7, was in reality a mounted and PTO-driven version of the MF721 but closely followed the model FF30 produced at the end of the TE20 era (June 1956 is the earliest reference I have). These early models had a latching device to take the weight off the hydraulic linkage once attached to the tractor and raised to its operating height. The short PTO shaft was telescopic and incorporated two Metalastic rubber couplings to take up misalignment.

The MF22-7, although very similar, did not incorporate a latching mechanism but had a conventional top link and relied on the position control facility of the MF35 or MF65 to maintain it in the fully-raised position. A conventional telescopic PTO shaft that incorporated a torque-limiting clutch was supplied with the machine, as were category I and II linkage pins. This arrangement enabled the hopper to be lowered for filling without having to remove the PTO, but in most cases bags of fertilizer were taken to the field on a trailer (the height of which was

A general view of the early Mounted Spinner Broadcaster FF30. Note the latching mechanism and the Metalastic joints on the PTO shaft.

The MF22-7 Mounted Spinner Broadcaster, showing the conventional PTO shaft. Above that is the anchor link that would only be used when coupled to a Ferguson TE20 tractor.

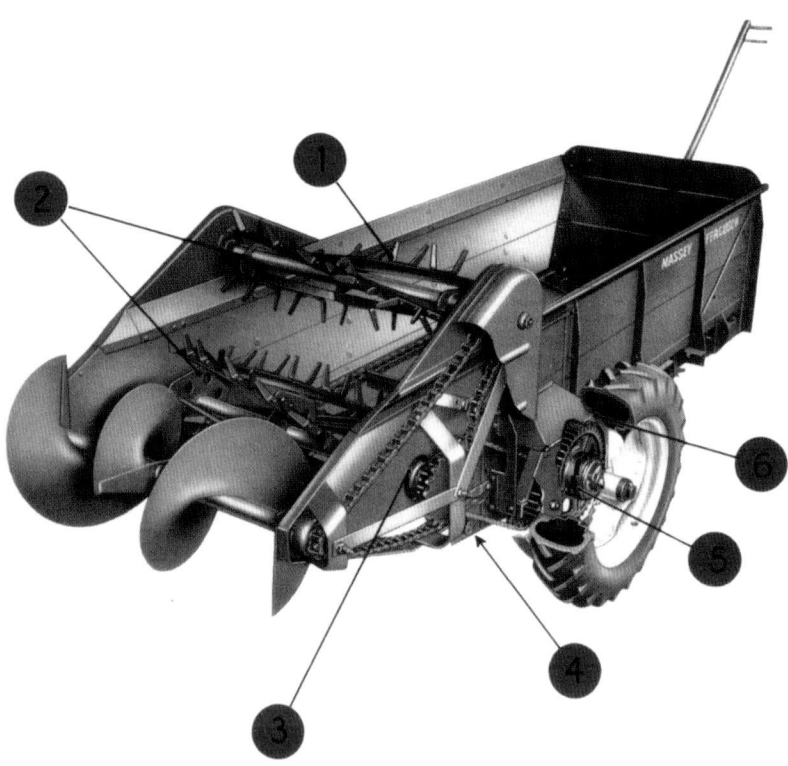

The MF712 Manure Spreader.
1. U-shaped teeth shred and throw manure in a wide even spread.
2. Unique "lawn mower" cylinder takes up load gradually. Note the bars follow a helical alignment.
3. Cylinder shafts are mounted on rubber-cushioned couplings for smooth operation.
4. Positive drive to cylinders and auger taken through strong chains all protected by a substantial steel cover.
5. Spring-loaded clutch to engage/disengage the drive.
6. Two-wheel ground drive means easy pulling and effective working in all conditions

generally ideal for tipping bags of fertilizer into the hopper). It was recommended that two stabilizers were fitted. An oil-filled bevel gearbox turned the drive through 90 degrees to turn the spreader disc at high speed and also provided the slower contra-rotation of the

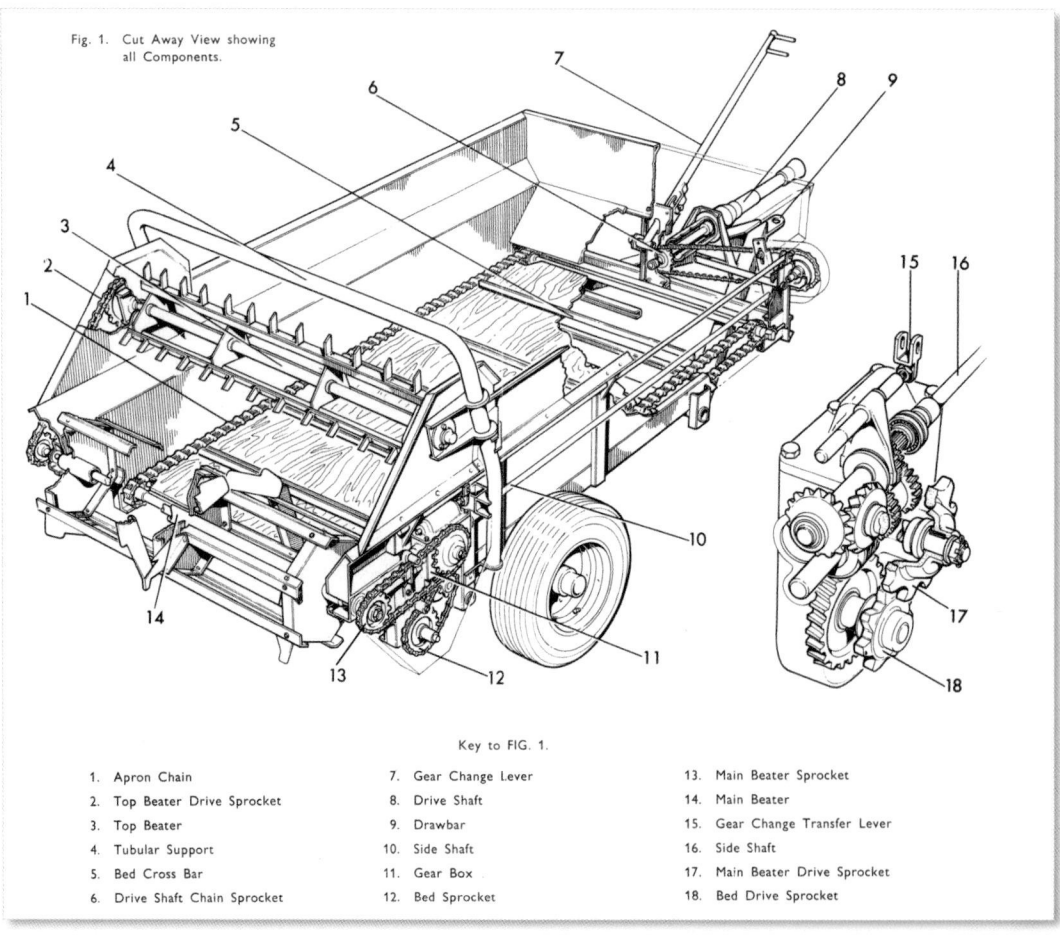

Sectioned drawing of the MF19-7 Manure Spreader, the 130-bushel version.

Fig. 1. Cut Away View showing all Components.

Key to FIG. 1.

1. Apron Chain	7. Gear Change Lever	13. Main Beater Sprocket
2. Top Beater Drive Sprocket	8. Drive Shaft	14. Main Beater
3. Top Beater	9. Drawbar	15. Gear Change Transfer Lever
4. Tubular Support	10. Side Shaft	16. Side Shaft
5. Bed Cross Bar	11. Gear Box	17. Main Beater Drive Sprocket
6. Drive Shaft Chain Sprocket	12. Bed Sprocket	18. Bed Drive Sprocket

agitator. Again, the top bracing tube within the hopper had a triangular spike welded to it, which served to speed up the opening of bags and obviated the need to use a penknife and the real possibility of losing it in the bulk of fertilizer! This spike may have been the subject of a patent application.

The MF712 Manure Spreader in reality came directly from the Massey-Harris drawing board, but had a modified drawbar offering either ring hitch with pan or a clevis drawbar with a built-in jack. The body was basically made of seasoned timber, the rear end being slightly wider than the front; this was to facilitate an easy feed to the spreader mechanism. The body had a capacity of 3920lb (1781kg) of wet manure. A double chain and slat conveyor on the floor of the spreader moved the material slowly towards the spreading mechanism at the rear. This was driven by a three-lobe cam on the left-hand wheel, the throw of which could be varied by a single control lever at the front of the machine within easy reach of the driver. The four settings on this lever gave application rates of 5, 10, 15 or 20 loads per acre. The right-hand wheel drove the spreading mechanism and was controlled by the same lever. Tyre sizes were 7.50x20, traction type. The body had an overall length of 8ft (2438mm) in size (front 38in (965mm), rear 40in (1016mm)) and a total unladen weight of 1496lb (679kg).

A more developed manure spreader, MF19-7, was introduced towards the end of the period covered by this book. The machine was PTO-driven and made in two capacities: the smallest was the 100 bushel (1.67cu.m), which had an overall width of 72in (1830mm), an overall height of 43in (1090mm) and an unladen weight of 1630lb (739kg). The larger spreader fitted with extension boards as standard was the 130-bushel (2.55cu.m) model, its width being 75.25in (1910mm), height 59.25in (1505mm), and weight of 1720lb (780kg). Both models were mounted on 9.00x16 multi-ribbed tyres. Only a clevis-type drawbar and jack were available. The machine was of all-metal construction.

Drive from the tractor was through a Walterscheid slip clutch mounted on the tractor end of the PTO shaft. The rear end fitted onto the main input shaft mounted centrally on the front of the spreader body; this carried a sprocket, which in conjunction with a roller chain took power across to a sprocket fitted at the front end of a

The MF732 Rear Mounted Mower.

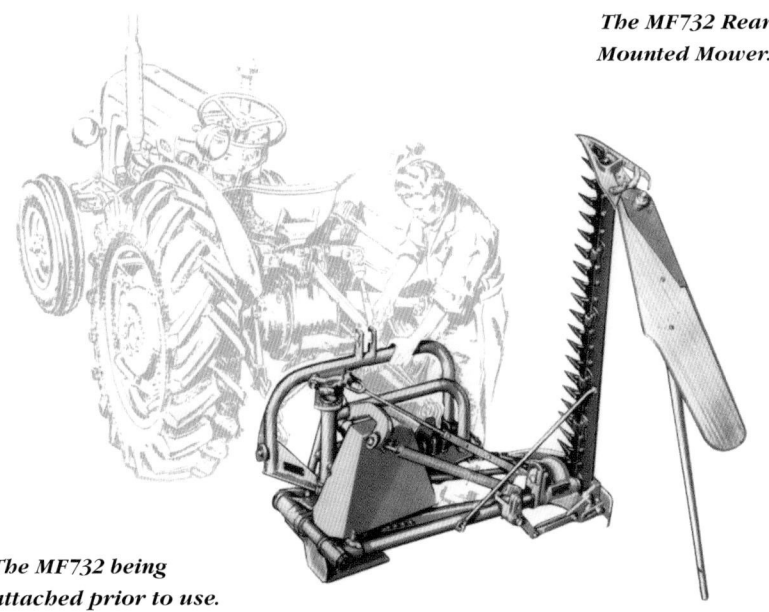

The MF732 being attached prior to use.

The MF779 Mid-Mounted Mower attached to an FE35 TVO model. Note the knife guard for safe transport. Fitted to the rear of the tractor is a Ferguson Side Delivery Rake D-EE-20.

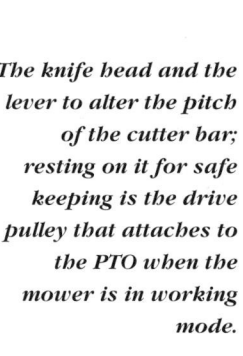

The knife head and the lever to alter the pitch of the cutter bar; resting on it for safe keeping is the drive pulley that attaches to the PTO when the mower is in working mode.

driveshaft on the right-hand side of the spreader, enclosed by a guard. This gave input to a gearbox mounted towards the rear of the machine. The gearbox provided two functions in the case of the 100 bushel model (ie drive to the bed conveyor and to the beaters), whilst on the 130 bushel model it provided the facility to have the choice of two different floor speeds; the change lever was positioned centrally at the front of the machine and was within reach of the driver. The two output shafts at 90 degrees to the centre line of the spreader were both fitted with sprockets: the top higher-speed sprocket transmitted drive by roller chain to the main lower beater; drive was then taken from the left-hand end of this shaft to the top beater (not fitted to the 100-bushel model). Drive to the moving bed was taken at a very slow speed via a roller chain and sprocket from the lower output shaft of the gearbox; as a protection device a shear bolt was fitted to the bed drive sprocket. The MF19-7 was a robust, tough and efficient spreader based, I should guess, on the output of American/Canadian Massey Ferguson engineers.

Hay and forage

Turning now to the range of hay and forage implements Massey Ferguson offered farmers in this period, the MF732 Rear Mounted Mower was introduced in the early part of 1962 as a replacement for the Ferguson rear mounted mower 5A-EE-B20. The MF732 was PTO-driven and linkage-mounted, being equipped with category I and II interchangeable linkage pins. The mower could be purchased with either a 5ft or 6ft (1524mm or 1830mm) reciprocating right-hand-mounted cutter bar. The frame of this mower was fabricated from tubular steel and had the usual break-back protection for the cutter bar. A unique feature of this machine was that it could be fairly easily altered to operate when coupled to a tractor with a wide track setting (such as 64in to 68in), which was a particularly safe and useful feature when cutting across a sloping field. Height of cut was achieved by setting the position control lever stop on the tractor's hydraulic system to give 19in (482.6mm) from ground level to the underside of the frame (being set parallel to the surface of the field). This was achieved by using the levelling box handle, then retained in place by a special sprung steel clip. A special position stop kit for use with the TE20 and David Brown 950 tractors was produced because these tractors did not have a position control function. In most other respects it followed the general arrangement used by other manufacturers but it was a popular mower in its day.

The MF779 Mid Mounted Mower was a new development designed to team up with FE/MF35 and MF65 tractors, but with appropriate fitting brackets could also be mounted on a TE20 tractor. This right-hand cutter bar mower was produced with either 5ft (1524mm) or 6ft (1828.8mm) sizes. Drive from the tractor's PTO fitted with a 9½in (241.3mm) diameter twin vee-belt pulley to a similar pulley but of 5in (127mm) diameter attached to a shaft at the rear end of a transmission tube running forward and parallel to the length of the tractor. The front end had a crank and balance weight attached, which drove the pitman and hence the knife of the mower; with these pulleys in place it gave a knife speed of 1077 reciprocations per minute. If a lower speed was desired, a smaller pulley could be fixed to the PTO to give 848 reciprocations per minute; both figures quoted were at the standard engine speed of 1500rpm.

The PTO shaft drive to the Side Delivery Rake as well as the pulley to take drive forward to the mower crank.

Left and below: Two rear views of the Ferguson Side Delivery Rake.

The MF736 Left Hand Mid Mounted Dyna-Balance Mower mounted on an MF35 tractor. It was specially developed for roadside mowing. Note the Dyna-Balance unit near the tractor with the hand lever for setting the knife-pitch.

In addition to the normal break-back protection for the cutter bar (similar in principle to that utilized on the MF732) these mid-mounted machines could be fitted with an extra safety feature that was brought into action if a cutter bar was to break back. It consisted of a Bowden cable anchored at one end to the clutch pedal by a special bracket, with the other end connected to the break-back strut. In operation, if the cutter bar struck an obstruction the Bowden cable pulled the clutch pedal down and thereby stopped the forward movement of the tractor. Two adjustments were provided for cutter bar height, regulated by skids at each end of the cutter bar to give either high or low settings. To some extent cutting height could be varied by altering the pitch of the bed in relationship to the ground. It would normally run parallel, but for laid crops the knife points would be set lower, whilst for use on stony ground they would be raised slightly. The adjustment was controlled by a lever and notched quadrant located at the inner end of the knife bed; four possible settings were provided. Lifting the cutter bar out of work was achieved by utilising the tractor's hydraulic linkage via a chain linkage fixed between the right-hand lower lift arm and the rear of the mower frame.

One of the great benefits of this mid-mounted position was that the tractor driver had an excel-lent view of what he was cutting without having to twist round in the seat. The other advantage of the mid-mounted layout was that quite a wide range of three-point linkage implements and trailers could be used with the mower still attached. Part of the standard equipment was a metal guard to cover the knife whilst being transported in the vertical position – a legal requirement for road use. From my experience, The MF779 was a nice mower to work with. Its weight with 5ft (1900mm) cutter bar was 380lb (172kg). It had a knife finger spacing of 3in (76mm) but a knife stroke of 3.2in (81mm), whereas both dimensions are usually the same.

A much more unusual machine was MF736 Left Hand Mid Mounted Mower, designed primarily for highway use so that the tractor followed the flow of traffic when operating on roadside verges. It was designed for use with the 35 or 65 but could be fitted to the TE20 series with the use of appropriate brackets. There were two salient features to this machine, the first being the ability of the cutter bar to be operated from 12 degrees beyond vertical to 45 degrees below horizontal. Please note that Massey Ferguson publications on this point varied. Either 3ft (914.4mm) or 5ft (1524mm) cutter bars could be specified.

The second important feature was found

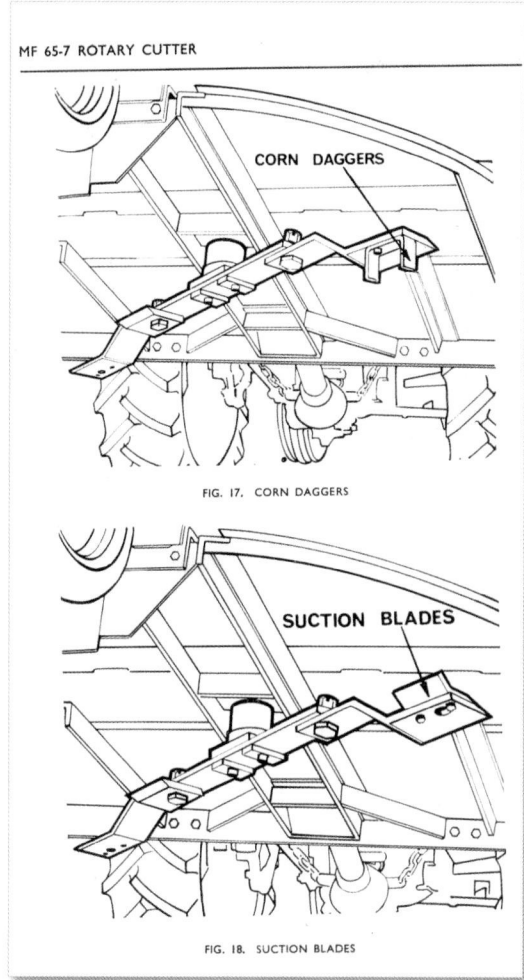

FIG. 17. CORN DAGGERS

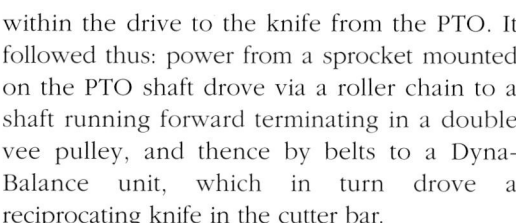

FIG. 18. SUCTION BLADES

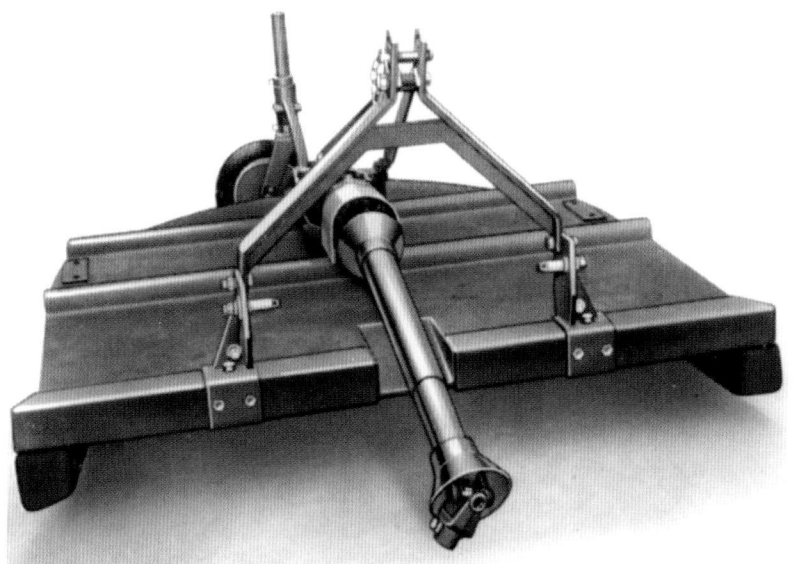

The blades available for the Rotary Cutter. Corn daggers are used to break up the stalks of kale, maize, etc, while suction blades create an updraught of air to lift any crop for cutting.

The MF65-7 Rotary Cutter. Note the lower link attachment pins are set for Category I.

within the drive to the knife from the PTO. It followed thus: power from a sprocket mounted on the PTO shaft drove via a roller chain to a shaft running forward terminating in a double vee pulley, and thence by belts to a Dyna-Balance unit, which in turn drove a reciprocating knife in the cutter bar.

The Dyna-Balance unit was protected by several patents, and being of an ingenious design it is worth considering in a little detail. The more traditional crank and pitman was a relatively crude method of converting rotary motion into a reciprocating movement to work the knife. The secret of the Dyna-Balance drive was that it was precision-made with counterbalance weights built in; the intention was to balance inertia forces set up by the reciprocating knife, thus achieving very low frictional losses and an almost silent and vibration-free drive. I can validate this by a little experiment I did with one of these mowers running while the tractor

was stationary. A full cup of coffee was placed on the bed of the knife – it remained in place and did not spill!

Having covered the drive system let us take a look at the three main control points of this unusual mower. The first was the manual setting of the knife tilt, which had a range of 20 degrees over seven stops of a hand lever. A pair of double-acting spool valves mounted on a bracket to the right of the driver close to the hydraulic quadrant controlled the other two functions: moving the right-hand lever to the rear lifted the mower bed so that it would clear kerbs; moving it forward would lower the bed The left-hand lever controlled the knife angle from just beyond vertical to below horizontal; again, rearward movement was for upwards, and forward movement lowered the angle of the knife. The earliest date of publicity material for this type of mower suggests that it was developed in America. These mowers were generally not used on farms but were popular with councils, golf courses and some industrial users.

A much less sophisticated machine was the MF65-7 Rotary Cutter, introduced to the implement range in 1957. These machines were linkage mounted but floated to follow ground contours with the aid of a trailing caster wheel. Both category I and II linkage pins were

The MF740 flail-type forager, showing both Offset and In-line versions.

The 441 Semi Mounted Forager.

The MF760 Offset Forager.

provided so they could be used with a wide range of tractors. To enable use with TE20 tractors a height-adjustment chain assembly and control rack had to be fitted to the top link, as well as a special PTO shaft with 1⅛in splined connection. These machines had a cutting width of 66in (1680mm) and a range of cutting heights between 2in (50mm) and 12in (300mm). Cutting height was set by first adjusting the rear single castor wheel to the desired height, then lifting the machine on the hydraulics until the body was level. Any slack in the support straps was taken up by adjustment of the chains and shackles anchored to the machine's gearbox mounting brackets. The cover of the rotating knife formed the main body of the machine, with the linkage attachment frame at the front and at the rear a single rubber-tyre caster wheel. Drive was taken from the tractor's PTO through a conventional jointed shaft fitted with a shear pin and safety pin at the input shaft of the right-angle-drive step-up oil-filled gearbox. A safety pin was incorporated which retained the coupling should the main pin shear. The vertical shaft, which extended under the body, had a flat

steel bar about 4ft (1219mm) long bolted to it; attached to the extreme ends of this bar by shoulder bolts were double-sided cutter blades. When both edges became blunt they could be sharpened – a good, economic design!

Two alternative blade attachments could be bolted on, increasing the versatility of the 65-7 Rotary Cutter. One type – known as corn daggers – consisted of a pair of extension knives that bolted below the existing blades at right angles. They were intended to be used for breaking up row-crop stalks of maize or kale. The other type – known as suction blades – were bolted to the top of the cutter blades and were designed to give an upward draught of air to lift laid crops for cutting. This was a useful and cheap general-purpose cutter, much copied today in a wide range of sizes and power requirements.

Forage

In the period covered by this book a rapid development of forage harvesters took place in Britain, but they had origins in America. Massey Ferguson, keen to offer farmers a choice of machines to match their needs, marketed at least five different types, each being described in order.

The MF740 In-line Forager and the MF740 Offset Forager both used the flail cutting principle, and had similar cutting widths and outputs, being 40in (1016mm) and up to 15 tons per hour depending on horsepower available. The rotor (to which 20 swinging flails were attached) revolved at 1400-1500rpm. Both machines were PTO-driven and trailed with a cutting height adjustable between 2in (50mm) and 12in (305mm).

The MF441 Semi Mounted Forager had a cutting width of 42in (1066mm) and a rotor equipped with 14 swinging flails. The advantage of this model was that, with the tractor equipped with its special tow frame on the three-point linkage, it was only necessary to remove the PTO shaft and take out one pin from the tow frame, leaving the trailer still hitched to the tractor's drawbar ready for transportation to the silo – a true one-man system. Alternatively, if two or more tractors were available, the driver could unhitch the loaded one for transportation to the silo; the empty trailer brought by the second tractor could be hitched to the forager and the combination could continue cutting.

A third type was the MF760 Offset Forager, which was designed for higher outputs achievable when coupled to the MF65 tractor. The cutting width of this machine was 58in (1473mm), again with a rotor speed in the range of 1400-1500rpm; it was equipped with 28 swinging flails. Massey Ferguson claimed this forager could harvest about 23 tons per hour depending on PTO horsepower available. These foragers could direct cut or pick-up from a cut swath.

The MF762 Chopper was in reality a combination of a 60in (1524mm) flail rotor equipped with 34 swinging double-ended flails. The cut material was fed into a cross-conveying auger running at 250rpm, feeding into a paddle fan with knives that chopped and blew the crop into a silage trailer either being pulled behind the chopper, or to the side if a tractor and trailer combination was travelling alongside. This was a much heavier machine than those described earlier. One of the great advantages of chopped silage was that it made for much easier mechan-

Fig. 2. Component Identification.

Fig. 3. Component Identification.

— 4 —

ical handling and feeding to livestock.

The MF37 Hay Conditioner was introduced to the range of implements early in 1963. At the time, crimping or conditioning of hay was a newish innovation to speed up the drying of hay crops. In principle the swath was passed between two contra-rotating fluted rollers, which were adjustable for clearance and timing, thereby

Explanatory illustrations from the instruction book for the MF762 Chopper.

The MF37 Hay Conditioner.

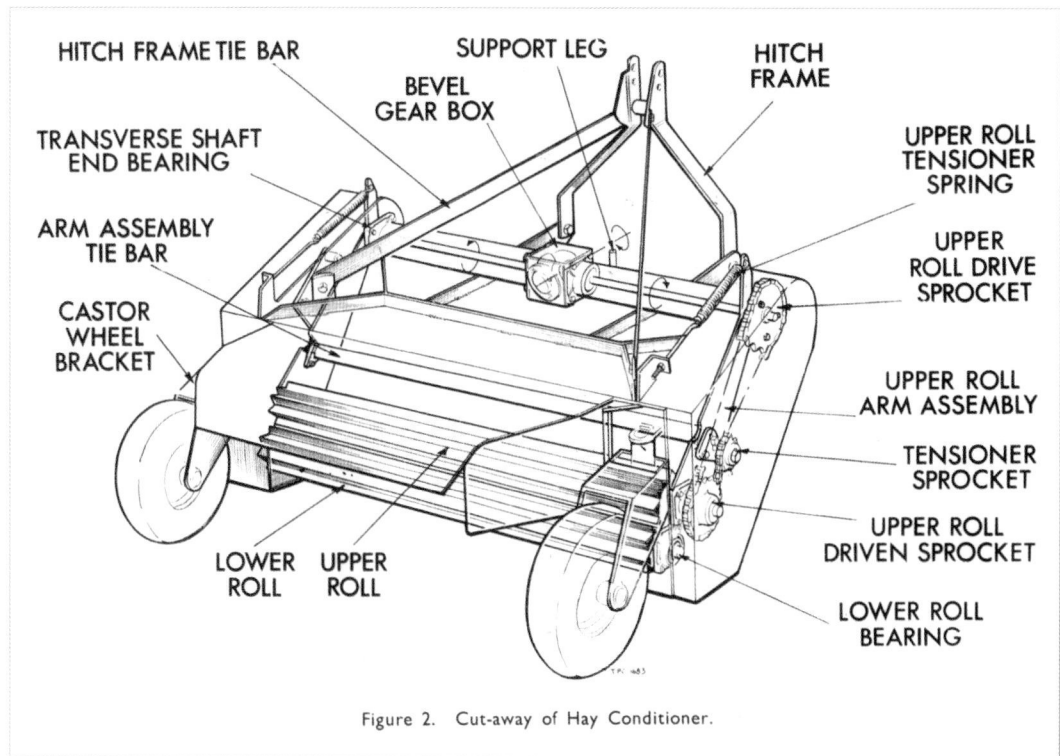

HITCH FRAME TIE BAR
SUPPORT LEG
HITCH FRAME
BEVEL GEAR BOX
TRANSVERSE SHAFT END BEARING
UPPER ROLL TENSIONER SPRING
ARM ASSEMBLY TIE BAR
UPPER ROLL DRIVE SPROCKET
CASTOR WHEEL BRACKET
UPPER ROLL ARM ASSEMBLY
TENSIONER SPROCKET
UPPER ROLL DRIVEN SPROCKET
LOWER ROLL   UPPER ROLL
LOWER ROLL BEARING

Figure 2.   Cut-away of Hay Conditioner.

The workings of the MF37 Hay Conditioner explained.

giving overall a wide range of crimping effect. The upper roller was spring-tensioned by an adjustable spring at either end of the roller's shaft. The objective when conditioning hay is to crack the stems and not to squeeze the moisture out, therefore the setting of the springs was to allow for different density and condition of crops.

The MF37 was PTO-driven and linkage-mounted (category I or II) with the use of pin sleeves, and had a pair of adjustable rear caster wheels to give variations in pick-up height. These hay conditioners could be used with any tractor equipped with three-point linkage and PTO. The MF37 operated in the following way: drive was taken from the PTO of the tractor through a conventional PTO shaft with a torque-limiting clutch fitted at the machine end; this fed power into a centrally-mounted right-angle-drive gearbox with contra-rotating output shafts extending to the left and right of the machine. These shafts had a sprocket fixed to each outer end, the left-hand side driving the lower fluted roller through a roller chain with a tensioning sprocket. The right-hand sprocket drove the upper fluted roller, again through a roller chain with tensioner but there was a facility on the roller sprocket to alter the timing of the flutes; three bolts were slackened off to alter the setting of the sprocket relative to the roller and then re-tightened.

The hay conditioner was intended to pick up a standard swath cut by a 5ft (1524mm) mower, which in reality gave a 4ft (1219mm) row of fodder. The top roller was 4ft 5in (1347mm) and had a diameter of 7⅜in (187.3mm) with 12 flutes, while the bottom roller was the same width but of 6⅜in (161.5mm) diameter with 10 flutes cut in. A convenient prop stand was fitted at the front of the machine and could be deployed when detaching it from the tractor.

It was suggested by Massey Ferguson that the hay conditioner should be operated at 4-8mph (6.5-13kph). The MF37 had an overall height of 3ft 5in (1041mm), width of 5ft 7in (1701mm), length of 4ft 10in (1473mm) and weight of 970lb (441kg).

A Massey Ferguson publication of the day claimed its machine had the following exclusive features:

i) The only conditioner with individual chain drive to the crimping rollers; this did not lacerate or shatter the crop.

ii) The only machine with adjustable roller clear-ance and timing; this allowed the widest variation in the intensity of treatment to suit the crop.

iii) The only crimper that was gentle enough to allow repeated processing of the swath, therefore reducing the curing time.

iv) The only crimper-type machine that was fully mounted on the tractor, which simplified operation and transportation.

In short, it was a well thought-out and well-produced implement of an innovative design.

Miscellaneous

In the final part of this chapter we will investigate the miscellaneous implements that were designed and marketed by Massey Ferguson during the period covered by this volume. A good many were carried over from the TE20 era, albeit perhaps with slight modifications but nevertheless well covered in the book *Ferguson TE20 In Detail*. The following list set out what miscellaneous implements Massey Ferguson salesmen had to offer customers, and is taken from a Massey Ferguson publication dated December 1962.

MF701 Transport Box
MF702 Transporter (larger than the MF701)
MF704 Linkage Winch
MF706 Earth Scoop
MF717 Three-ton Tipping Trailer
MF720 Cordwood Saw
MF721 Multi-purpose Blade
MF723 Post Hole Digger
MF737 Forklift
MF718 Buck Rake (10- and 12-tine models)
MF728 Potato Spinner
MF760 Hydrovane Compressor, 60cfm
Tyre tracks (no number)
MF719/720/721 Low Volume Sprayer
MF25 Hydrovane Compressor, 25cfm
MF Kale Cut Rake

Various other items of equipment were introduced to complement the MF35 and MF65, and were not carryovers from the TE20 era. The first to come to mind is the MF18-7 trailer, which had a rated carrying capacity of five tons (5080kg); Massey Ferguson claimed it could carry more but did not specify! This trailer was made in either fixed or tipping versions, although needless to say the latter was by far the more popular. In their construc-

This MF sales leaflet gave an idea of the range of augers available. It omits to mention that the 2 cutting blades secured with three bolts are also replaceable.

The MF723 Post Hole Digger attached to an MF35X Vineyard tractor. Note the slip clutch on the PTO shaft.

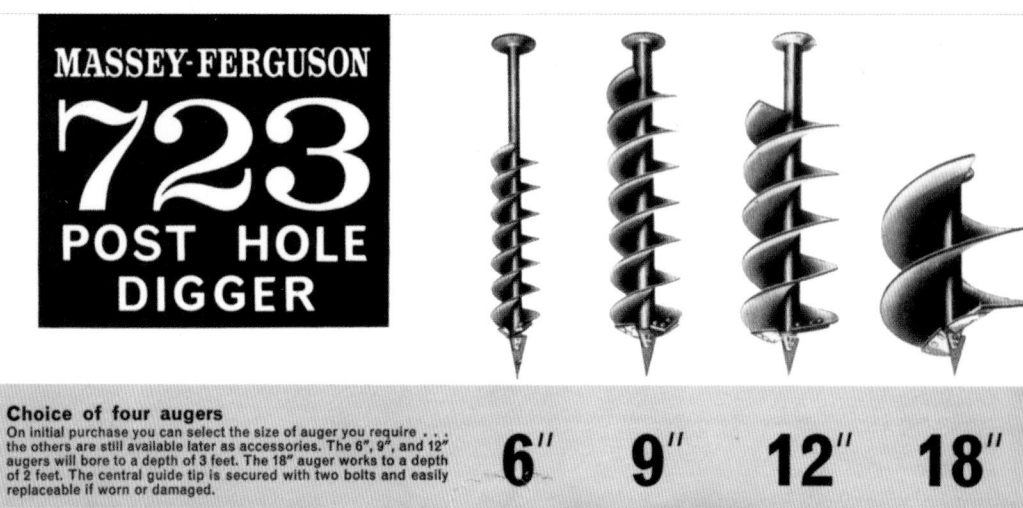

MASSEY-FERGUSON 723 POST HOLE DIGGER

Choice of four augers

On initial purchase you can select the size of auger you require . . . the others are still available later as accessories. The 6", 9", and 12" augers will bore to a depth of 3 feet. The 18" auger works to a depth of 2 feet. The central guide tip is secured with two bolts and easily replaceable if worn or damaged.

6"   9"   12"   18"

tion the trailers were enlarged and strength-ened versions of the MF717 three-ton trailer but the head, side and tail boards were of all-steel construction: the side boards were made in two sections with a central removable pillar, which made for easier handling. The overall dimensions were 16ft 10in (5130mm) length and width of 6ft 4in (1930mm), with an internal body size of 13ft 1in (3988mm) length, width of 5ft 10½in (1791mm) and depth of 1ft

An MF35 and and MF171 3-ton trailer with rear body extension and hay ladders fitted.

To illustrate the MF18-7 5-ton trailer, I have used this photograph taken from a Dealer Product Information sheet dated February 1963.

Economical handling of GREEN CROPS..

... with the MASSEY-FERGUSON 718 BUCKRAKE

★ Convenient for operator handling, the trip mechanism is designed for efficient working even under full load.

Collect, carry, and unload the easy way! With the 718 Buckrake, these three tasks can be combined into one simple speedy operation, giving you easy and economical handling of silage, hay and fodder crops.

Also, those out-of-season jobs such as the movement of grain sacks, straw bales, poultry houses, and boxes, may be easily handled by this versatile implement, which carries a maximum load of 12 cwts. and has a normal working capacity of 750 lbs.

A choice of two models, 10 or 12-tine, are available with similar lifting capabilities. Both fit all Ferguson System tractors and certain Category 2 tractors as well.

Short tines are available if required. They are 3 feet long—give a 32% increase in tipping angle enabling you to discharge the load easily on soft clamps.

4in (406mm). Tipping trailers could be tipped to an angle of 54 degrees.

Unlike the MF717 three-ton trailer, the larger MF18-7 had only one fixed position for the axle that carried the wheels, which were shod with 12x18 eight-ply tyres. The brakes were internal expanding with 11x2¼in (279.4x57mm) drums, mechanically operated by a hand lever within reach of the driver and able to be locked on for parking. The timber used for the floor of the trailer was tongue-and-grooved Keruing, a quality hardwood. To widen the range of tractors that this trailer could be coupled to, an interchangeable drawbar end was provided as either a ring hitch with detachable support pan or a clevis type, used in conjunction with an adjustable screw jack.

Hay lades of all-metal construction for the front and rear were produced as accessories, but special brackets needed to be welded to the trailer to enable fitment. Grain extension sides were also available, which doubled the capacity of the body; they were formed along similar lines to the lower panels. An interesting feature (at the time) was built into the top-hung rear tailgate. This opened automatically on tipping the body, but when fully lowered it became positively locked.

The final implement to be considered in this chapter is the FE35 or MF735 Loader, which was first produced with the advent of the FE35 tractor. It could be mounted on MF35s or MF65s and, with the use of appropriate brackets, Massey Ferguson claimed it could be fitted to the TE20 range – but this was a most

Opposite: The MF718 Buckrake.

The MF Kale Cut Rake, an implement unique to the MF range invented by a farmer to save time on that horrible winter job of cutting and carting kale!

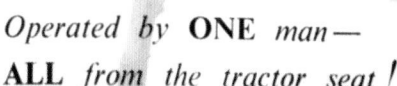

unusual combination! The loader attachment basically consisted of five fabricated units: the loader frame, built up using tubular steel sections; a rectangular box section bolted to four tapped fixing holes under the clutch housing and extending either side by about 12in (300mm); a pair of tubular side frame assemblies bolted either side of the transmission casing, secured to the top of the transverse box section at the front, with the rear ends connected to special brackets attached to the rear fender bolts; hydraulic rams either side of the tractor (the lower fixed end of each cylinder pivoted on a pin at the forward end of the side frame, while the telescopic end attached by a pin to the main loader frame; both sides were similar); the fifth element was the loader front end attachment, of which several types were available.

The basic fork was made to trip manually and self-return, or it could be fitted with a hydraulic push-off plate. The forks had eight high carbon steel tines of 1in (25.4mm) diameter. The manual fork was 43in (1066mm) wide, while the hydraulic version was 48½in (1232mm) wide. Two types of buckets were offered, again either with manual trip and spring-assisted return, or a hydraulically-tipped type, and both buckets had approximately the same dimensions – a capacity of 10cu.ft (0.28cu.m) and a width in the region of 43in (1092mm). A dozer blade at 5ft 6in (1676mm) wide was made, which could be supplied with a pre-set manual adjustment or the ability to be altered hydraulically. A root fork, which was only available in a trip-operated form, was

produced, being 59in (1498mm) wide with a capacity of 12.5cu.ft (0.35cu.m). The forks were of tubular steel construction, with tines set at 4in (101mm) centres; they featured rounded ends to prevent them from damaging roots. A pallet fork tipper was also made to fit the MF735 Loader. It had hydraulic angling, and it was ideal for handling stillage boxes containing root crops.

As a tailpiece to this description of the MF735 Loader a further essential accessory was required: the fitment to the tractor three-point linkage of the standard Massey Ferguson automatic hitch. This fulfilled three functions. First, it ensured the satisfactory working of the loader; with the hitch in place it limited the height to which the lift arms would rise, thereby ensuring there was a supply of hydraulic oil under pressure to operate not only the loader but also to tip a trailer body. It also, of course, provided a convenient point on which to hang the rear concrete counterbalance weight of 560lb (254.5kg), which was an important aid to traction and lighter steering! The pick-up hitch hook made coupling and uncoupling of trailers and muck spreaders a truly one-man operation.

In conclusion, although there were slightly fewer types of implements marketed during the period covered by this chapter than the range produced during the TE20 era, they nevertheless sold extremely well. No doubt this was because they were designed in-house to be operated by Massey Ferguson's own two models of tractor, and as such were tailor-made with a high regard to specification and performance.

Left: The MF735 Loader, a very popular machine in its day, with all the elements of the frame clearly shown.

Chapter Six

Accessories and Conversions

The accessories described in this chapter were all the products of Massey Ferguson engineers, designed to enhance the operational efficiency of their tractors and implements. Some accessories have already been described where it seemed appropriate alongside the relevant tractor or implement text, so they will not be considered again here. In the latter part of this chapter we will look at some of the conversions offered by outside manufacturers for the 35 and 65.

For the FE35 and MF35, a kit of parts known as Universal Category I and II Linkage was available. It comprised a pair of lower links each fitted with a category I ball to one end and a category II ball to the other, plus two bushes of the correct size to be used on the implement end when a category I implement was attached. For hitching a category II implement, the bushes were not required. The top link kit consisted of three elements, each a flat bar of high-carbon steel with adjustment holes along the centre line. At the end of each bar was a swaged-in

ball. Two of these bars had category I balls, while the other had a category II ball. They could be bolted to form a top link of the desired configuration and length.

As mentioned earlier, the automatic pick-up hitch was a carryover from the TE20 era, but a swinging drawbar kit was also marketed for the 35 and 65 (on MF65 MkIIs it became standard). The swinging drawbar provided certain advantages over the earlier flat nine-hole type with stays, generally used on early FE35 tractors.

The advantages were as follows: it did not occupy the tractor's three-point linkage, so that the whole drawbar assembly could remain in place while a linkage implement was attached; it was readily adjustable for height and could be set to either side of the centre line; and the main benefit came to the fore when using a trailed PTO implement in that the distance between the drawbar pin and the PTO shaft was 14in (356mm), and thus to the SAE standard.

A combination support bracket adapted the tow hook to match both the automatic hitch and the swinging drawbar. Stabilisers and suitable axle brackets continued to be offered, but for use with the MF65 a special type was produced incorporating a turn-buckle and lock nut to provide adjustment. They were attached to the lower links near to the rear ends by engaging with a short pin. To enable MF65 MkI tractors to pull category II implements if they were originally equipped with category I ball ends, a kit was offered to meet this requirement; it was

The fixed hitch, which is a rare find today, taken from the February 1963 MF Accessories list.

Fixed Hitch

Provides an exceptionally rigid hitch point for trailed—especially PTO driven—heavy implements and preserves full ground clearance.

standard on MF65 MkIIs. A fixed hitch was manufactured, which fitted the 35 and 65. It was of heavy construction.

An Increased Lift Linkage kit was produced for the MF65, primarily intended for use with the heavy MF85 three-furrow plough. This simple kit consisted of a pair of triangular metal plates, each attached with two bolts to each of the lower lift links, with a hole at the apex providing an attachment point for the lift rods; as this point was nearer to the mounted plough, extra leverage was gained for lift but the lifting height was slightly reduced.

By 1961 Massey Ferguson had designed and marketed an aid to traction that enabled MF65 tractors to operate trailed equipment more effectively. It was known as the Multi Pull Hitch. The main frame of this piece of equipment fitted to the three-point linkage in the normal way: at the

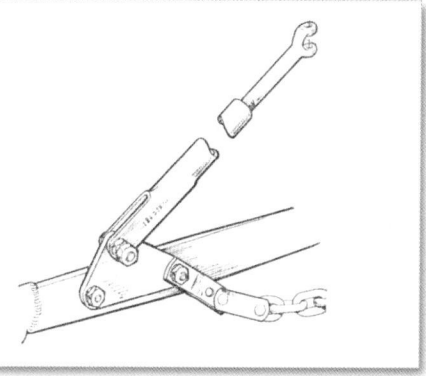

Increased Lift Linkage

Triangular plates bolted to each lower link provide alternative attachment point for lift rods. Effects increased lift capacity at ends of lower links. Primarily intended for use with M-F 85 3 furrow Reversible Plough.

top and rear of this frame was a slightly curved tubular bar. On top of this bar ran a guide wheel, and a stirrup was suspended from its centre, which in turn had a heavy but adjustable chain attached. When a trailed implement or trailer was hitched to the tractor's drawbar this

The Increased Lift Linkage, taken from the Accessories list.

SIMPLE 3-POINT MOUNTING

The Multipull Hitch is attached to the 3-point linkage. It is fitted in seconds.

ATTACH THE DRAWBAR

The drawbar of your trailed implement is coupled to the hook under the rear axle. Slip in a pin and you have a strong, universal joint.

READY FOR USE

That's all you have to do—the Multipull Hitch is ready for work.

And here's a remarkable feature of the MULTIPULL HITCH! Even on undulating ground the grip is constant.

If the tractor rides over a mound, the two-way hydraulic system *exclusive* to Ferguson System tractors automatically compensates. The whole linkage moves to take up the change in position, but the weight transference is never altered. Again, if the tractor enters a depression, the same thing happens.

So your tractor and implement will keep moving steadily, no matter how rough the ground.

The Multi-Pull Hitch was designed for the MF65. Transferring weight from the trailer to the tractor's rear wheels resulted in much improved traction.

The Dowty oil pipe kit fitted to an MF35.

Power steering was available on both the MkI and MkII MF65, and could be specified on a new order or fitted retrospectively by a Massey Ferguson dealer. The oil pressure pump was directly driven off the timing gears of the engine. The ram and shuttle valve controlling the power assistance was concealed behind the radiator grille; the normal mechanical steering linkage was retained, so it was failsafe. To drive a tractor in those days with power steering would have been a real luxury, yet today we all take it for granted!

As in the TE20 era, a belt pulley was included in the accessory line-up, specially engineered to accept the 1⅜in PTO shaft found on the 35 and 65. Even a sleeve was made to reduce the internal diameter to 1⅛in for TE20 tractors. As mentioned in Chapter Four, a more robust design of belt pulley was made for use with MF65 tractors, able to cope with the extra horse-power. It also incorporated a quick-release facility.

Various models of differential lock were available, including one for retro-fitment to earlier FE35s, up to serial number 283319; these tractors were not originally designed to have this feature fitted as an option. Later tractors had provision for the fitment of a differential lock but it was not standard equipment, although it became standard on the MF65 MkII. As for a differential lock being fitted as standard on MF35Xs, there seems to be a conflict within published Massey Ferguson brochures – two, both dated December 1962, disagree on the point. There is an opinion that diff lock was standard on very late three-cylinder 35s and most 35Xs unless a special order was placed for a non-diff lock tractor.

Tyre tracks similar to those available for the TE20 range of tractors continued to be offered, but only for MF35 models. These gave greater flotation and traction over sand, soft boggy ground or deep snow; they also found wide use in forestry work with their ability to climb over roots and fallen branches.

During the period covered by this book Massey Ferguson introduced the option of power-adjustable variable track wheels (generally referred to as PAVT wheels), suitable for use with MF35s. These rear wheels offered power adjustment within two ranges, each with an intermediate setting of track width, thus 48-64in (1219-1625mm) and 60-76in (1524-1930mm).

chain would be wrapped around the implement's drawbar. With the position control lever set to fast response, the draft control lever was raised to give more traction. In operation this obviously tended to raise the front of the tractor, so Massey Ferguson recommended the fitment of front weights to gain extra traction!

An oil pipe kit (often known as a trailer tipping pipe) was available to take off hydraulic pressure for tipping trailers, etc. Two types were produced, each tailored to the relevant model. They had either the smaller Dowty coupling or the larger Exactor-type coupling – whichever suited the farmer's needs.

This concept came from the design offices of Allis Chalmers and for a time was the subject of a patent.

The principle by which this system worked was that the wheel centre could screw itself in or out of the wheel rim to a limited extent under the power of the tractor! This was achieved by having four short, curved, square steel bars (known as rails) welded to the inner side of the rim to form a helix; four clamps were bolted to the wheel centre, each equipped with a locking cam, tightened or released by a special square socket spanner. One of these bars on each wheel had holes drilled through to allow clamp-type stops to be positioned at predetermined points, thus giving an intermediate track setting to the figures quoted above. It was a most worthwhile addition to a tractor that needed to have its track altered frequently and easily without jacking the wheels clear of the ground.

A dual rear wheel attachment kit was carried over from the TE20 days and was suitable for the MF35. An enlarged version was produced for use with MF65 tractors, featuring wheel studs of a larger pitch diameter. The kit consisted of special wheel nuts (eight per wheel) with thread extensions that protruded through the thickness of a cast circular spacer plate, which had holes to line up with the tractor's wheel studs. The tractor's original wheel nuts were used to hold the second wheel in place against the spacer. The second set of rear wheels was not included in the kit.

Wheel girdles were also carried over from TE20 days. They were easy to fit and a highly effective means of improving traction under slippery conditions. Often, when ploughing, it was only necessary to fit one to the left-hand rear wheel. Small cast steel spade lugs could be bolted to the cross bars if extra grip was needed, but they were suitable only for the 35. Steel rear wheels with bolt-on lugs were available in two sizes, suited to either the 35 or the 65.

A tractor jack, operated by the tractor's own hydraulic lift, continued to be available (albeit in a slightly modified form) and could be used with the 35 or 65. The stand placed under the front axle support casting had a screw-adjustable spike that located into a pre-drilled hole (only on the 35). A special version was made to operate with the MF65 High Clearance model.

A wide range of cast-iron wheel weights

continued to be offered for users needing more traction or better stability. Front wheel weights were available for the MF35 Vineyards, for MF35s with 19in or 16in wheels, and for the MF65 with 16in wheels. Weights were available for the rear of the 35 with 28in wheels. For the MF65 two different kits were produced: the first kit was more expensive but was a necessary addition before a second or subsequent set could be fitted.

Also to add weight to the MF65, but this time at the front, a weight frame could be fitted. It incorporated a draw clevis, and up to eight detachable weights (known as jerrycan weights or suitcase weights) could be added to the frame as required. Each weight was 60lb

Part of an MF leaflet, the only one available, to illustrate the PAVT, or power adjusted, wheels.

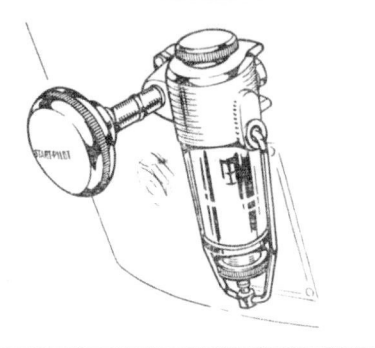

Hand Brake Kit

For '35' Tractor ratchet type hand lever is linked to the existing brake system—operates independently of foot pedals. For '65' tractor similar hand lever operates drum type wheel assemblies additional to and completely separate from the existing transmission disc brakes.

Start Pilot Kit

Cold starting aid suitable for '35' Tractors with 23C Diesel engine. Comprises pump incorporating capsule holder mounted on instrument panel and metal tube leading to a nozzle fitted in the rubber hose between the air cleaner and inlet manifold. Speeds up the get-away on cold mornings.

Front weights fitted to an MF65.

The Dual Spool Valve Kit provides hydraulic control over two remote single-acting hydraulic cylinders.

(27.2kg), so in total 480lb (218.18kg) could be added plus the weight of the frame, making a total addition of 525lb (265.2kg).

The MF35 and MF65 MkI did not have lighting as standard equipment, but the MF65 MkII did. So to address this omission, Massey Ferguson produced lighting sets comprising two headlights with double filament bulbs, which could be mounted on the top of the bonnet (when a loader was fitted) or (generally) on brackets either side of the bonnet; on MF65 MkIs they were usually bolted directly to the sides of the bonnet. On top of each rear

The Hand Brake Kit and the Start Pilot Kit for the FE35 four-cylinder diesel engine.

mudguard was mounted a combined front and rear marker light, as well as a red reflector. A number plate mounting bracket complete with its own lamp and a two-pin trailer socket was included in the kit. A single ploughing lamp, incorporating its own switch, could be mounted on the right-hand mudguard as an extra. How users' expectations have been extended since those times!

If growers wanted to upgrade the instrumentation on a basic 35 Vineyard model by the fitment of a tractormeter, it was available in two forms – one calibrated to give correct road speed when 9.00x24 rear wheels were fitted, the other the standard type when 10x28 wheels were fitted.

For MF35 tractors a ratchet-type handbrake lever kit was offered. It was linked to the existing system, but independently of the foot pedals; in 1963 it cost £9.17s.2d. The handbrake version for the MF65 was much more expensive (at £53.0.0) because its installation necessitated the fitment of a drum brake assembly to each rear wheel hub, as featured on the Industrial MF65 MkII.

In an attempt to improve the poor cold starting characteristics of FE35s built using the Standard 23C diesel engine a cold-start pilot kit could be fitted. This comprised a capsule holder

Dual Spool (Weston) Valve and Selector Valve

The dual spool valve provides hydraulic control over two remote single acting hydraulic cylinders. The selector valve provides a means of controlling single acting hydraulic cylinders from the tractor hydraulic quadrant. It can be used in conjunction with the dual spool valve to provide a means of control for three single acting hydraulic cylinders.

Two Spool Valve and Combining Valve

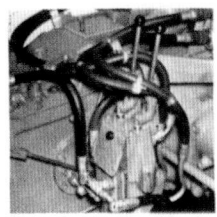

The two-spool valve mounted on the left-hand footrest can be used to control two single or double acting remote hydraulic rams.

The combining valve provides a means of uniting the flow of the tractor hydraulic pump with that of the high capacity auxiliary pump. This ensures faster response when operating remote hydraulic cylinders.

and a small hand-operated plunger pump which enabled ether contained within the capsule to be injected into the air intake manifold via a metal tube leading to a nozzle set within the rubber air intake pipe. The pump was mounted on the instrument panel; was this an early form of Easy Start?

As mentioned in the chapter on implements, a dual spool valve kit was produced, to be bolted directly to the top of the hydraulic cover in place of the transfer cap, which gave control over two single-acting remote rams. A selector valve could be added to the dual valve to give control over a third remote ram. This accessory was required when operating a Massey Ferguson MF711 potato harvester, for example.

Canvas tractor covers continued to be available, designed to fit any 35 or 65 model.

To improve the comfort of drivers who had a standard 35 with a pan seat, Massey Ferguson marketed a complete Deluxe seat as a replacement.

Conversions

Conversions of all the tractors covered in this book were produced by outside manufacturers, so let us first consider those designed to improve traction by driving all four wheels. Selene of Northern Italy was well established in this area, and had produced a four-wheel-drive conversion for the TE20 and other makes. It was therefore natural that with the introduction of the FE35, and later the MF65, Selene would produce conversions for these models though they used a different system.

It may be worth pondering a moment on the trading relationships surrounding Selene, Roadless Traction and Four Wheel Traction, all of which were involved in promoting four-wheel-drive conversion kits for a variety of makes of tractors. Dr Sion Segre-Amar, together with a short-term partner, established a business in Nichelino, near Turin, in Northern Italy just after the end of World War II to import second-hand tractors (mainly Fordsons and Fergusons) from

The Fuller family's MF35 four-wheel-drive conversion, which is on loan to the Coldridge Collection.

The longest wheelbase ever, on the Fuller-owned MF35. To the rear of the standard gearbox are a Fuller creeper gearbox and the transfer box for the 4WD conversion.

The massive front axle.

Four Wheel Traction also marketed power steering kits, which in reality were essential when a tractor was converted to 4WD.

The reduction hubs are most vulnerable to the ingress of dirt; perhaps sealing caps were once fitted.

England. The tractors were then refurbished, often with new Perkins diesel engines (for which Dr Sion Segre-Amar was the main agent in Italy, trading under a different title). It has been suggested that he chose the name Selene for his business because it was the name of his wife; he later chose his son's name Manuel for the four-wheel-drive conversion kits. A real family man!

Very early on, Segre-Amar decided to develop a four-wheel-drive system for Fordson, Ferguson and some other continental makes. The first he developed was known as System 1, and eventually there were four others; their differences lay in the way drive to the front axle was picked up from the existing transmission. System 1 was used on Fordsons and Ferguson TE20s, and consisted of a sandwich transfer box installed between the gearbox and back axle housing. Within this transfer box was a sliding gear operated by a hand lever, which enabled two- or four-wheel drive to be selected. The output shaft of the transfer box to the left-hand side of the tractor was connected by a Hardy Spicer shaft to the drive pinion of the front axle. The axles were sourced from ex-army vehicles – Jeep for Ferguson TE20s and GMC for Fordsons, MF35s and MF65s.

Phillip Johnson, then managing director and chairman of Roadless Traction, had been heavily

The neat power steering pump, driven directly off the timing gears.

This is the MF35 High Clearance model produced by F Staden. The front wheels are standard 400x19 whilst the the rears are 600x38. The rear- and mid-mounted hoes are made by Nicholson for working sugar beet.

involved in long-term development of track-laying systems for a wide range of applications since 1919. By 1952 Johnson had met up with Segre-Amar while in Italy, and eventually reached an agreement between the two firms that Roadless Traction could manufacturer Selene Manuel conversions under licence, but only for Fordson tractors (all of Selene's four systems were protected by patents).

System 4 was developed to allow a four-wheel-drive conversion to be fitted to certain Landinis and Fiats, alongside MF35, 65, 130, 135, 165 and 175 tractors. This system exploited the fact that these Massey Ferguson tractors all had ground-speed PTO as well as the usual engine-speed PTO. Selene decided that by fitting a transfer box with the facility to disengage the output drive by a hand lever, this box coupled directly to the tractor's PTO shaft, which meant a saving in cost and installation time could be achieved.

It so happened that Robert Eden had established a business in 1948 to buy second-hand tractors from around Britain and export them to other countries, but a high proportion were sent to Selene for refurbishment and were often converted to four-wheel drive. By 1950 William Fuller had joined the company of Robert Eden. Two years later he bought the company but continued to trade under the original name. Fuller felt it worthwhile to offer Selene Manuel four-wheel-drive conversion kits for his farming customers' Massey Ferguson tractors, and imported them from Italy. By 1956 he had fitted a Selene Manuel System 4 conversion to a FE35, and more followed, both for the 35 and the 65. In due course he became concerned that the Selene transfer box was not robust enough, so he produced a strengthened version. Although outwardly very similar the two 'boxes can be easily identified: the earliest type had Selene cast into the rear cover plate, while the later, stronger type had RE cast into it.

The main drawback to the System 4 was that if four-wheel drive was in use it precluded the operation of the PTO in the normal way. An extension of the tractor's PTO passed through the casing of the transfer box so that PTO implements could be operated, but not when four-wheel drive was engaged. Outside the remit of this book but nevertheless worth noting is that by 1968 Fuller had reached an agreement with Segre-Amar to manufacture a sandwich-type transfer box designed by Fuller himself, thus getting around the drawbacks of System 4. This became the foundation stone of a new business William Fuller set up in 1965, known as Four Wheel Traction.

An unexpected addition to this chapter has recently come to light as a result of the researches of Phil Homer, webmaster of the Standard Car Club. He discovered photographs of an auxiliary power unit (APU) mounted on what was obviously a modified FE35. The photographs, along with drawings and limited information, were found in the archives of the Heritage Motor Centre museum at Gaydon, Warwickshire. Phil submitted the find, together with explanatory text, to *Old Tractor* magazine, which published the story early in 2011. What follows is my interpretation of that article, together with input from people knowledgeable of aviation and gas turbines; units of this type were known colloquially as huffers.

The running gear was clearly based on an FE35 Industrial diesel tractor (note the hand-brake lever and battery on the nearside in the accompanying picture) but the front hubs, front wheels and rear wheels were clearly of Vineyard specification – smaller than normal. The front grille was obviously FE35, as were the rear-view mirrors, dashboard and lighting equipment. If the rear-mounted fuel tank came directly from a Ferguson medium-pressure crop sprayer, it had a capacity of 92 gallons (418 litres), and would feed the Standard Motor Company gas turbine mounted underneath the bodywork, adjacent to the right-hand side of the tractor. Note that this vehicle was not symmetrical.

The gas turbine would be started by an electrical starter, possibly powered by the tractor's batteries, perhaps boosted by having the tractor's engine running and hence the dynamo charging. As can be seen to the right-hand side of the driver's seat, there was a control panel for the turbine. Starting turbine engines of civil and military aircraft in the mid-1950s generally required input from this kind of auxiliary power unit. At the time, Standard produced gas turbine engines under licence from Rolls-Royce at its Fletchampstead North factory in Coventry. These engines were sometimes fitted to Meteor jet fighters and to Comet passenger airliners.

Tony Lee, an ex-employee of Standard Motor Company remembers an APU or huffer being installed in a Standard Atlas van and being used to start a Russian aircraft, presumably at the Midland airport. The mode of operation was as follows: a tapping was taken off the compression stage of the APU turbine, fed into a 3in or 4in flexible hose, which was in turn connected to the starting input socket on the engine being started. To achieve this, a relatively high volume of air was needed but at a pressure of about 40psi – enough to bring a build-up of 40 per cent within the turbine being started before the heat and then the fuel was fed in. In contrast, most modern aircraft turbine engines have their own built-in starting facility.

This particular APU seems, as far as Standard was concerned, to be something of an experimental unit but nevertheless an unusual adaptation of an FE35. Needless to say, the author was fired-up (pun intended) by the discovery of the photographs!

The Auxiliary Power Unit, mounted on a modified FE35.

Chapter Seven

Overseas

The centre spread of a late 1990s TAFE (Indian) brochure showing the models they were then producing.

This chapter is based totally on information I have been able to glean from three people directly involved with Massey Ferguson overseas operations, namely Jeremy Burgess (one-time licensee director at AGCO), John Farnworth (who worked in Saudi Arabia during production of the 35 and 65) and Bob Dickman (who worked in Europe and Scandi-navia for Massey Ferguson during those times). Their stories will unfold in the following pages. Unfortunately, contributions from South Africa, Pakistan and India are limited to period photographs and some production figures.

Here we'll let Jeremy Burgess outline the framework within which Massey Ferguson operated overseas.

THE **UNBEATABLE RANGE**

Harry Ferguson had clearly shown a remarkable vision in the Ferguson Brown Model A and subsequent Ford Ferguson and TE20 ranges. The vision was for a fully-integrated farm mechanisation solution that combined man, machine and implement into an efficient and reliable unit. The single objective was to facilitate the production of affordable food for the growing world population.

The TE20 had really proved the value of this concept, and with more than 500,000 TE20s produced in England alone, a very significant volume had been exported – not just to the developed markets of Europe and North America but to many far-flung and emerging agricultural economies in the Middle East, Asia, Africa and South America.

Commercially successful and punching well above its weight in the field, the TE20 was an iconic machine. However, it had its limitations, specifically in the areas of transmission hydraulics and PTO. The four-speed transmission lacked a slow enough forward speed for use with powered cultivation machinery, such as the rotavator, which in the 1950s was gaining in popularity. The hydraulic system had limited lift capacity and lacked position control (the ability to hold a mounted implement at a fixed height above the ground), and the PTO and hydraulic system had no so-called live drive – a facility allowing forward motion to cease but with PTO and hydraulic power remaining running. These factors, together with the modest power output of Standard engines, meant the TE20 was no longer the machine needed to carry on the development of world agriculture that it set out to achieve.

The advent of the FE35 and later MF35 addressed all of the issues defined above. More power came from the Standard 23C engine and later the Perkins A3.152. The six-speed transmission gave a wider spread of gears, including slower forward speeds. A dual clutch provided live hydraulics and PTO, and the hydraulic system lift capacity and operating pressure increased. Position control became standard fitment, as well as Ferguson System draft control.

Collectively these features transformed the tractor into a machine with significantly more performance and capability. Its abilities were particularly welcome in the developing parts of the world, where agriculture often involved breaking new ground and working in very arduous conditions. The 35 quickly established itself in export markets, and with the global distribution network combined from the Ferguson and Massey-Harris companies, orders quickly rolled in.

The Massey Ferguson distribution network was by now the most comprehensive in the world. The network was made up of two basic concepts: one for markets where Massey Ferguson operated distribution on a national basis, and in turn appointed dealers to retail machines to end users (these were markets like the UK, France, USA and Australia, where Massey Ferguson had a manufacturing presence, although not solely limited to them); the other was for markets where a national distributor or importer was appointed. This distributor would retail machines to farmers, either through its own sales branches or through independent dealers around the country. This latter model was the case in Africa, the Far East, Middle East and some parts of Europe. In addition, Massey Ferguson opened a number of regional representative offices where regional sales and service staff were based. Offices existed in places such as Kenya, Beirut and Singapore. Massey Ferguson was then present in about 150 countries.

Around the time of the MF35 and 65, the concept of licensing the design for local assembly and ultimately manufacture was a very active business concept. Some significant agricultural economies existed in countries that in some cases were closed to conventional imports. A local assembly operation helped overcome these restrictions, and as a result reduced import duties were paid.

Massey Ferguson and its sister company Perkins were very active in the field of licensing. The early sixties saw the signing of licence agreements for the MF35 in India, Pakistan (both still active today), Turkey and Yugoslavia, and the MF65 in Brazil. This opened the door to significant volumes and also helped relieve the pressure on the very stretched Banner Lane factory in Coventry.

In practice a licence agreement allowed the licensee to import tractors in CKD (completely knocked down) form and assemble them. Subject to a tightly defined deletion process, the licensee could gradually begin to manufacture components locally, these parts then being deleted from the kit supplied from Coventry. The components chosen for deletion would usually be dictated by a combination of local manufacturing capability, along with the commodities that attracted the highest import duties in the given country.

Before a part was accepted for deletion the licensee would submit a detailed report on their manufacturing capability of the part, together with samples for testing by Massey Ferguson engineers in the UK. The concept was that ultimately the licensee could become the sole source of a particular component and actually supply it back to Massey Ferguson for use in Banner Lane. In practice this rarely happened in the early days of license agreements.

It is important to note that a CKD tractor was not one that had been built up and then knocked down for shipping – this was known as PKD, or partly knocked down. Machines in PKD condition were sent to many more markets than those covered by the official licensing agreements, PKD usually being a means of minimising shipping costs through reducing the cube of the unit rather than a means of developing local production.

In contrast, a CKD tractor was essentially supplied as several boxes of bits that had never been assembled; some assemblies were sent built up (like the engine, the complete gearbox or rear axle), the remaining parts being shipped loose in packages ready to go onto the licensee's assembly line. A large CKD department existed at Banner Lane to supply and pack

the kits for licensees, with the monitoring of the list of parts and ongoing deletion process being a very involved job. CKD kits were usually supplied in what were known as cycles, which were usually multiples of 8, 16, 24, 32 or 64 units. As a kit's content got smaller typically the cycle size got bigger.

The business concept planned for a new model to be introduced and licensed by the time an existing machine was fully localised, thus refreshing the process and prompting everything to start all over again. In practice, the durability of the design of the MF35 in particular was such that many years later the same basic machine is still in production in several of the countries mentioned above.

India was one of the largest licensee operations, the license for the MF35 tractor being signed between Massey Ferguson and Tractors and Farm Equipment (TAFE) in 1960. Interestingly, Simpsons Engines – a TAFE sister company – was already an established Perkins Licensee making the P3 and P6 engines. This resulted in the TAFE-built MF35 having a P3 engine fitted rather than the 3.152. Although Simpsons later took on a 3.152 licence, the firm continued with the P3 for many years. The last P3-engined MF35 came off the line in Chennai in 2002 when the introduction of engine emission regulations in India finally brought about the end of P Series engine production.

The MF35 three-cylinder differed very little in principle from its successor the MF135, which in turn evolved into the MF240. This tractor and endless detailed variants of it are still in production today. Indeed, at the time of writing in 2011 there will be in excess of 150,000 tractors of this same basic design built this year alone, particularly in India and Pakistan where the MF240 and variants are a staple machine of agriculture and

The TAFE factory at Sembium, Chennai. Mr Browning of TAFE, who supplied the accompanying photographs, recollects, "On one occasion I delivered a batch of these tractors to the Indian Army at their depot near Chennai. There was quite a crowd of army personnel standing around, most of whom were from the Punjab, a major farming area. One of them told me, with a lot of personal pride and affection, "Yeh toh sone ki chidiyan (These are golden birds)." What a positive validation of their humanitarian worth!

Final stages of assembly. Note the hand brace and the Esso diesel pump.

even road haulage. In India it is common for an MF240 to operate at train weights of over 25 tons on road haulage. In a recent test, an MF240 manufactured by TAFE in India successfully pulled a train of sugar cane trailers -weighing 120 tons - along a 20km journey to a sugar mill!

Total production of MF35 and MF65 tractors and their variants is difficult to estimate, but it runs to several millions. When the last tractor rolled off the production line in Banner Lane on 24 December 2002, Banner Lane had supplied 3,307,996 tractors or tractor kits. The large quantities of tractors made by licensees without kit content from Banner Lane must be added to this figure, together with production from other Massey Ferguson facilities worldwide.

It is therefore not an exaggeration to say that there is no other tractor design in history that has contributed more to the feeding of the world's population than the MF35 tractor and its subsequent variants. A very bold statement, but true. If Harry Ferguson were alive today he could take great satisfaction from the fact that his vision of providing affordable food for the world's population through effective mechanisation has moved a long way towards fulfilment.

Yes, that was Harry Ferguson's vision, but let us not forget that it was Harry Ferguson's chief engineer, Herman Klemm, in North America, who developed the basic TO20 into the TO35, the concepts and engineering of which were very closely followed and incorporated into the FE35. It is recorded that when Harry Ferguson was introduced to this model at his home, Abbots Wood, he was most disparaging of what he saw.

John Farnworth has written 12 books on the history and products of Massey-Harris, Ferguson, Massey-Harris-Ferguson and Massey Ferguson, covering aspects of design, manufacture and marketing, not only of the tractors but also of their associated implements. What follows is a distillation by the author of John's experiences of using these tractors as a student in North Wales, and later in several different research centres in Saudi Arabia.

John's father was a farmer and vegetable grower, based on the edge of Manchester, with his uncle farming the adjacent holding. John's first encounter with tractors was learning to drive a 1939 Massey-Harris 12-20, soon followed by a 1948 TEA.20. This was followed by an MF35 bought second-hand with a 23C engine. Being a bit heavier than the TEA.20 it was popular with the family for ploughing and heavier field work. Sadly, due to its biggest weakness – poor cold-starting characteristics, despite repeated attempts by the local Massey Ferguson dealership to rectify the issue – it had to be tow started each winter morning by the TEA.20! Nevertheless, it proved to be totally reliable in every other aspect, including driveability, which was sheer bliss even with oil fumes puffing out through the engine's breather!

This tractor was used so extensively that the linkage balls wore out and had to be replaced. The twin six-volt batteries with their flat terminals were difficult to keep free of corrosion.

Another gripe that John found from experience, and this also applied to the TEA.20, was the design of the rear wheel centre-to-rim attachment bolts. As vegetable growers they had to alter the track setting frequently. The fine threads would quickly rust up and the nib holding the bolt head to the wheel centre would round off. The Farnworths overcame this problem by changing the bolts to a conventional type, with a coarser thread, spring washer and a smear of grease! John recalls once hauling a four-wheeled trailer loaded with bags of barley, and stalling the MF35 engine – the batteries refused to start it, but he successfully restarted it by resorting to hand cranking!

John's next experience was with an MF35 fitted with a Perkins A3.152, which he bought on behalf of his father from the University College of North Wales farm, where he was a post-graduate student. It had done a lot of work but was a tidy tractor, having been used mainly for ploughing and forage carting duties; just prior to purchase the farm manager informed John that the tractor's hydraulics did not work, which no doubt improved John's bargaining power. On getting the tractor back to his father's farm, the transmission dipstick was checked – there was no oil showing, so they refilled it to the correct level and the tractor worked for evermore.

Father and uncle went on to acquire two more of the three-cylinder MF35s, which gave sterling service for many years, but they were particularly conscientious about checking the tightness of the four nuts that attached the pick-up hitch to the axle casing, keeping the front tyres up to pressure and keeping an eye on the front wheel bearings. The last purchase made by John's father was of an ex-Eccles Parks Department FE35, painted green. It was a superb starter and had a high-ratio top gear – maybe a US-specification overdrive and top gear. John's father and uncle retired in the early 1990s.

In 1970 John went to Saudi Arabia as manager of a large experimental farm. Finding the farm to be short of tractors, he acquired four or five 23C-engined 35s from defunct government farms. All had been abandoned due to neglect and petty bureaucratic resistance to obtaining spare parts. They had been sand-blasted by the desert storms. These tractors were soon resurrected by fitting new tyres. With good batteries almost unobtainable, John thought it prudent to buy hand-cranked starters from Lucas UK, which bolted directly in place of the electric versions. The principle of these machines was that a large spring inside the casing was wound up by a cranking handle set at 90 degrees to the centre line of the tractor; when fully wound the tension was released to rotate the pinion that engaged with the flywheel, thus starting the engine. Simms, which produced injection equipment, manufactured a similar product, known as a Simms inertia starter.

John's first encounter with MF65s was at the university farm, prior to which the largest tractor

This photograph taken by John Farnworth gives a good indication of the arid conditions under which man and machine had to work.

Swath turning the Saudi way. Note the overhead protection for the driver.

he had driven was a Fordson E27N. So the MF65 was a revelation! It always worked hard at ploughing and forage harvesting duties, as well as lighter work. The driver Gwynfor Williams had nothing but praise for the tractor, and particularly liked its stability when ploughing mountain slopes in North Wales.

When John moved to work in Saudi Arabia he acquired four MF65 MkIIs, all in reasonable condition, from other government farms. Two were immediately set to work running 24 hours a day (only stopped for refuelling) to drive water pumps via their PTOs. John found the PTO clutches wore out fairly rapidly on this duty, but heavy-duty clutch plates were listed in the parts book, so they were duly sourced and fitted – and there was no reccurrence of the problem. These tractors were working under constant load at up to 120 degrees Fahrenheit in the shade! They worked hard, were completely overhauled every winter, and never had any PTO drive problems.

The other two MF65s were used every day on fertilizing and hay harvesting work. They had their own dedicated drivers, Abdullah and Saad, who really liked the machines. Because of the arid conditions, routine oil and filter changes were done at half the recommended time spans; oil was cheap in Saudi! John comments, "That they all performed so well in this arid environment and with first-generation Saudi mechanics does, I think, speak louder than words of their innate good design and high build quality." They had a few problems with the dry disc

One of John's early tractors baling.

brakes but he liked the fact that they were easy to drive and to hitch implements to.

When John left his assignment in Saudi Arabia six years later, all the 35s and 65s were still going strong but the farm had added four MF165s to the fleet. The government had sent them a supremely gutless Ford 5000 and two clumsy, heavy International B614s, which Saudi drivers disliked intensely.

Massey Ferguson had great success with sales in Saudi as its agricultural revolution took off in the late seventies and early eighties, and eventually a Massey Ferguson tractor assembly plant was established there.

In his work in Saudi Arabia managing the

An MF 65 driving the laboratory's generator.

A rather battered MF65 on the experimental farm.

Retired Massey Ferguson employee Bob Dickman shares with us some of his experiences with Massey Ferguson during the production run of the 35 and 65.

It had been Bob's original intention to become a farmer, and with that in mind he undertook a one-year National Certificate training course at the Newton Rigg College of Agriculture in Cumbria. But a change of circumstances took him, in 1955, to a successful interview for a post as an instructor at the Massey Ferguson training school in Stoneleigh. After his initial indoctrination in all things Ferguson and the necessary training for him to fulfil this new role, Bob started his working life at Stoneleigh. His mentor was the late Keith Base, a most kind and charming man, an ex-WWII Spitfire pilot who was shot down over the Sussex coast and severely burned but luckily pulled out of the burning wreckage by farm workers.

Early in Bob's time at Stoneleigh, working as a trainee instructor and still in his blue overalls, he had his first contact with Harry Ferguson, who noticed a small speck of oil on Bob's overalls. Harry said quietly, "Laddy, I would get yourself a clean pair of overalls as soon as possible." This comment left a lasting impression on Bob, and illustrated Harry Ferguson's concern with detail and perfectionism in everything and everybody connected with the Ferguson image.

One of the dedicated tractor drivers on his MF65 tractor. Note the New Holland baler.

Bob Dickman during his days at Stoneleigh Abbey as an instructor.

Hofuf Agricultural Research Centre, John always used Massey Ferguson implements wherever possible. These included MF721 Grader, MF728 Chisel Plough, MF738 Tiller, MF Border Ridger, MF51 PTO Drive Mower, MF25 Side Rake, MF12 Baler and MF22 Fertilizer Spinner, along with a considerable range of other British manufacturers' implements.

John's concluding observation: "Treat the 35s and 65s well and they will repay you handsomely in terms of work and pleasure, just as they did when first produced nearly 60 years ago."

Bob driving a petrol-engined FE35 at the Horse of the Year Show at Haringay North London in 1956. Note the embellishment on the bonnet front.

Bob worked first as a training instructor on the TE20 range of tractors and implements, but within a short space of time moved to work on evaluating a new training scheme to enable instructors to teach students the workings of FE35 tractors and their range of implements, which were to be introduced to the farming community on 1 October 1956. Particular reference was given to the then-new CAV distributor-type fuel injection pump and also the two-lever hydraulic control system, embracing both draft and position control. Also given special attention were the workings of the two-stage clutch that was fitted to Deluxe models. Bob, like Keith, was a privileged member of a small, dedicated team who trained Edmund Hillary (later Sir Edmund Hillary) and his men on the workings of the three TE.A20 tractors that made their epic journey from Scott Base to the South Pole from 1957 to 1958.

In 1960 Bob was transferred to Massey Ferguson's export service department, working under Charles Voss; more training followed to enable Bob to become conversant with that department's internal workings. Following another successful spell of training he was given his first export assignment, working alongside

Massey Ferguson sales manager Jaap Vogelsang on the Massey Ferguson stand at the Leipzig Fair in East Germany, where the then-new FE35 was given its first European showing. This early experience in the export market taught Bob that quite frequently one had to 'oil some wheels' in order to secure certain business and to get things done!

As an aside, Bob recalls the time when their

Bob's Commer support van being loaded on to a Silver City Airways Bristol Freighter at Lydd airport, Kent, heading for Le Touquet in France.

This photo taken at a Leipzig Fair is of the East German President admiring the MF 135 on the display, with the local MF dealer looking on.

teristic of the 23C engine, particularly in Switzerland where temperatures of minus-10 to minus-20 degrees centigrade were quite common. They tried, with some success, heavier battery cables, ether starting aids and individual glow plugs in each combustion chamber, as well as the use of lower-viscosity engine oil (SAE 5W/10). In the field they frequently had to visit farmers to explain the use of the two-lever hydraulic controls. Bob was also expected to have a good understanding of Massey Ferguson combines and balers because the MF630 combine was very popular, particularly in Austria.

As service representatives Bob and his colleagues were expected to carry out many functions. One was to enhance distributor/dealer development by raising the standards of after-sales service. This was achieved by advising on correct workshop facilities, including special tools, Massey Ferguson signage, service vans and the equipment they were expected to carry. Likewise, they had to ensure high standards of customer care and the proper commissioning of new machines. They were to investigate service and product failures, gathering sufficient evidence and samples so that issues could be analysed and hopefully dealt with by Massey Ferguson engineering and quality control departments; this work also meant carrying out warranty audits to ensure

Standard Vanguard car broke down, suffering a fractured fan blade in the no-stopping zone between West and East Germany. After a quick stop to remove, by primitive methods, the opposite blade, they continued their journey without being arrested by East German guards.

Their main concern on the technical side was trying to deal with the poor starting charac-

Sorting a combine problem somewhere in Austria. Note the Perkins badge on the front of the Commer van.

that claims submitted by distributors were correct under the terms of the Massey Ferguson warranty scheme.

As the FE35 evolved into the MF35 with the Perkins A3.152 engine, many of the earlier problems disappeared and this range of tractors became well accepted. With the demise of the LTX project, the Massey Ferguson marketing men were desperate for the introduction of the long-awaited MF65, which came about in December 1957.

Its popularity was rapidly established in Bob's territories. The later MkII model fitted with the more powerful direct-injection Perkins AD4.203 considerably enhanced the appeal of this range of tractors in November 1960. Shortly afterwards, Bob was promoted to service manager covering the three Scandinavian countries plus Finland. In these areas many Massey Ferguson dealers had produced their own specialised equipment to fit the MF65, including full- and half-tracks, forestry equipment, diggers, front loader and such like. It fell to Bob's team to ensure these designs were approved by the Massey Ferguson engineering offices at Maudslay Road in Coventry, where it could be established that they did not overload the tractor.

Bob remembers one trip to the most northerly town in Finland, Ivalo, about 150 miles north of the Arctic Circle, where they were testing logging attachments for the MF65. Winter temperatures were minus-45 degrees centigrade, and there were about three hours of semi-light each day. To ensure the tractors could be successfully restarted each morning, the oil was drained and the batteries removed to be taken indoors overnight. They lived in log cabins on a boring diet of reindeer meat, potatoes and milk, and alcohol was forbidden. The only relaxation was an extremely hot sauna each day, followed by a roll in the snow or a plunge into a hole cut in the ice to cool off!

In total, Bob worked for Massey Ferguson for more than 40 years, and I must quote verbatim Bob's final sentence of his story. "Having visited 110 export countries and been deeply involved with the launching of the 35, the 65 and subsequent models, I would like to dedicate some of the success of these products to three loyal Massey Ferguson employees: Peter Delingpale, Erik Fredrikson and Keith Base. Each, in his own particular area of expertise, did so much to foster the good reputation that the 35/65 range earned."

Chapter Eight

MF35 and MF65 in use today

Roger Hill's tractors still going strong after half a century: a team of three MF35s, with an MF135 joining in, harvesting reed on a hot day in Devon, 2011.

As is well known, TE20 tractors are still able to prove themselves to be useful little workhorses, meanwhile providing pleasure to those who use them in a recreational context.

However, the MF35 and, to a lesser extent, the MF65, find a much wider application today,

especially on smaller farms and with hobby farmers, as well as with those who participate in ploughing events and tractor road runs. It is worth reflecting for a moment on the reasons for this wide and continuing usage, of the MF35 in particular. Both the 35 and 65 represented a major evolutionary development of

the one-time revolutionary Ferguson System embodied in earlier models. Let us consider what these improvements were, which will in turn highlight the reasons for their continuing popularity today.

With the introduction of the 35 in 1956, the compactness of the TE20 was retained. The wheelbase of the new model was only 2in (50mm) longer but eventually, with the introduction of the MF35X, the power output had risen to 41bhp at the PTO (the earlier TE20 developed only 26bhp at the PTO) and there were much improved torque characteristics.

Another major development was the availability of six forward gears and two reverse, and later the option of Multi Power, which gave 12 forward speeds. The overall top speed was about the same as the TE20 on the standard 35 model, but the lower ratios enabled an implement such as the Howard Rotavator to be successfully used without retro-fitment of a creeper gearbox or the Ferguson epicyclic gearbox. Thus the 35 in its standard form was able to deal with a much wider range of applications.

The other significant and much appreciated refinement was the introduction of position control on the hydraulic lift while still retaining the Ferguson System draft control. This allowed the operator to choose the most appropriate hydraulic control system for the task in hand. Coinciding with this improvement was a general strengthening of the hydraulic components, as well as a useful increase in available hydraulic pressure. Another important improvement over the TE20 range was the fitting of an SAE six-spline 1⅜in PTO shaft, making it compatible with a wide range of suitably-scaled farm implements produced by manufacturers around the world today.

The relative simplicity of these models (apart from the fuel injection equipment) is an endearing factor, which means any competent DIY mechanic can deal with all normal servicing and running repairs in his own workshop. AGCO still markets a range of replacement parts for these models (components they do not supply are generally well catered for by a wide range of specialist suppliers, usually at very keen prices), so for anyone contemplating a small tractor for smallholding, ploughing days or road runs, what better choice than an MF35X?

For people who own a TE20, 35 or 65, two

clubs have been established, facilitating the sharing of problems and solutions and thereby expanding the collective knowledge. Within this framework a more general social backdrop has been developed, manifesting itself in diverse ways such as the organisation of road runs, ploughing events, stalls at local tractor rallies and extended annual AGMs On a broader front, numerous tractor magazines cater for the wider tractor preservation scene.

Finally, just to validate the usefulness of the 35 today, it is worth reiterating the point made in Chapter Three that close modern variants of the 35 are still produced at factories in Pakistan, India and Turkey.

Appendix A: Serial numbers FE35, MF35, MF65

Production figures taken from Massey Ferguson publications.

Date	Serial numbers: FE35/MF35
1956	1001 - 9225
1957	9226 - 79552
1958	79553 - 125067
1959	125068 - 171470
1960	171471 - 220613
1961	220614 - 267527
1962	267528 - 307230
1963	307231 - 352254
1964	352255 - 388384

Note: I was told on good authority that the red and grey paint
came in on number 74656.

Production figures taken from Massey Ferguson publications.

Date	Serial numbers: MF65
1958	500001 - 510450
1959	510451 - 520568
1960	520569 - 533179
1961	533180 - 551732
1962	551733 - 552234
1963	552235 - 593027
1964	593028 - 614024

Appendix B: Prefix letters used by Massey Ferguson on the MF35 and MF65

First letter	Prefix letter
Normal Width Agricultural	S
Vineyard	V
Industrial	I
High Clearance	C

Second letter	Prefix letter
Petrol engine, 6:1 compression ratio	G
Petrol engine, high altitude 6.6:1 cr	H
Diesel engine 23C	D
TVO engine	K
Lamp oil engine	L
Perkins diesel engine A3.152	N

Third and subsequent letters	Prefix letter
Single clutch	F
Dual clutch	M
Diff lock	Y
Multi Power	W

Appendix C: First build dates, FE35 & MF35

First of each model built from 1956, FE35/MF35

Year	Model	Code	Serial No	Date Built	Comments
1956	FE35	SDF	1002	Wednesday 27 August	Std Diesel 23c single clutch
1956	FE35	SDM	1001	Wednesday 27 August	Std Diesel 23c dual clutch
1956	FE35	SGM	1201	Friday 7 September	Std Petrol dual clutch
1956	FE35	SGF	1365	Tuesday 18 September	Std Petrol single clutch
1956	FE35	SKF	2016	Friday 5 October	Std TVO single clutch
1956	FE35	SKM	2013	Friday 5 October	Std TVO dual clutch
1956	FE35	SHM	2012	Friday 5 October	Std High Altitude dual clutch
1956	FE35	SLM	2079	Monday 8 October	Std Lamp Oil dual clutch
1956	FE35	SLF	5381	Friday 23 November	Std Lamp Oil single clutch
1956	FE35	JGF	6538	Tuesday 4 December	Industrial Petrol single clutch
1956	FE35	JDM	7515	Thursday 13 December	Industrial Diesel 23c dual clutch
1957	FE35	JDF	12477	Wednesday 23 January	Industrial Diesel 23c single clutch
1957	MF35	SNF	18182	Friday 1 March	Std Perkins 3 cyl single clutch 1st 3cyl MF35
1957	FE35	JGM	21847	Monday 25 March	Industrial Petrol dual clutch
1957	MF35	JNF	40315	Friday 21 June nightshift	Industrial Perkins 3 cyl single clutch
1957	FE35	YDF	44462	Tuesday 9 July	Vineyard Diesel 23c single clutch
1957	MF35	SNM	45952	Monday 15 July	Std Perkins 3 cyl dual clutch
1957	MF35	JNM	46238	Tuesday 16 July	Industrial Perkins 3 cyl dual clutch
1957	FE35	VKF	54185	Thursday 29 August nightshift	Vineyard TVO single clutch
1957	FE35	VGF	57033	Tuesday 10 September nightshift	Vineyard Petrol single clutch
1957	FE35	VDM	61862	Monday 23 Septernber nightshift	Vineyard Diesel 23c dual clutch
1957	FE35	JKM	65939	Thursday 17 October	Industrial TVO dual clutch
1957	MF35	VNF	66438	Monday 21 October	Vineyard Perkins 3 cyl single clutch
1958	FE35	VKM	97895	Friday 25 April	Vineyard TVO dual clutch
1958	FE35	VGM	97897	Friday 25 April	Vineyard Petrol dual clutch
1958	FE35	SHF	101017	Monday 19 May	Std High Altitude single clutch
1958	FE35	VHF	110815	Thursday 21 August	Vineyard High Altitude single clutch
1958	FE35	VHM	114547	Tuesday 23 September	Vineyard High Altitude dual clutch
1960	MF35	VNM	175731	Monday 25 January nightshift	Vineyard Perkins 3 cyl dual clutch
1960	MF35	VDM	181083	Wednesday 2 March	Last 23c Diesel MF35
1962	MF35	SNMY	285565	Wednesday 23 May nightshift	Std Perkins 3cyl dual clutch 1st diff lock
1962	MF35	SNFY	285623	Wednesday 23 May nightshift	Std Perkins 3 cyl single clutch diff lock
1962	MF35	SKFY	286756	Thursday 31 May nightshift	Std TVO single clutch diff lock.
1962	MF35	SKMY	287883	Wednesday 13 June nightshift	Std TVO dual clutch diff lock.
1962	MF35	SHMY	289051	Friday 22 June	Std High Altitude dual clutch diff lock.
1962	MF35	SNMYW	2890B0	Friday 25 June	Std Perkins 3 cyl dual clutch diff lock 1st MultiPower
1952	MF35	SHFY	291565	Monday 30 July	Std High Altitude single clutch diff lock
1962	MF35	SGFY	295935	Thursday 6 September nightshift	Std Petrol single clutch diff lock
1962	MF35X	SNMY	302413	Thursday 8 November	Claimed to be the 1st MF 35X would also be 1st with diff lock
1962	MF35X	SNMYW	302458	Thursday 8 November	Believed to be 1st 35X MultiPower if above true

Appendix D: Build dates, MF65

First of each model built from 1958 MF65

Year	Model	Code	Serial No	Date Built	Comments
1958	MF65	SN	500001	Tuesday 11 March	1st MF65
1556	MF65	SNY	501043	Wednesday 7 May	1st MF65 with diff lock
1958	MFB5	CNY	505941	Wednesday 23 July Nightshift	1st High Clearance MF65 with diff lock
1958	MF65	CN	507766	Tuesday 23 September Nightshift	1st High Clearance MF65 Basic model
1960	MF65	SNDY	531453	Wednesday 9 November	1st MkI Direct injection engine
1960	MF65	CNDY	532081	Thursday 1 December	1st High Clearance MF65 Direct injection MkII with diff lock
1960	MF65	SND	531678	Thursday 17 December	1st MkII Direct injection without diff lock
1960	MF65	CND	532779	Tuesday 20 December Nightshift	1st High Clearance MF65 Direct injection MkII
1961	MF65	JM	543923	Thursday 17 August	1st MkII Industrial
1961	MF65	JMY	543920	Thursday 17 August	1st MkII Industrial with diff lock
1961	MF65	JAY	544153	Tuesday 22 August Nightshift	1st MF65 Industrial MkII tractor Instant reverse
1961	MF 65	JA	545646	Monday 18 September	1st MF65 Industrial MKII with diff lock Instant reverse
1962	MF 65	SNDYW	554963	Monday 27 August	1st MkII with MultiPower .
1962	MF 65	CNDYW	568078	Tuesday 16 October nightshift	1st MkI High Clearance with MultiPower

Appendix E: Last build dates

Last of each model built

Year	Model	Serial No	Date Built	Comments
1957	**FE35**	SDF 74655	Monday 2 December 1957	
1960	**MF35 4 Cylinder**	VDM 181083	Wednesday 2 March 1960	
1964	**MF35**	388382	1964	No records for last tractor built
1964	**MF35X**	Not known	1964	No records for last tractor built
1964	**MF65**	614024	1964	No records for last tractor built

Appendix F: Comparisons

TRACTOR COMPARISON — 35X AND COMPETITORS (taken from MF publication dated 1962)

MAKE		M-F	FORD	FORD	I.H.C.	I.H.C.	DAVID BROWN	NUFFIELD	ALLIS CHALMERS
MODEL		35X	Dexta	Super Dexta	B 275	B 414	850	342	E.D.40
WEIGHT	pounds	3192	3318	3343	3460	3613	3750	4330	3,80
WHEEL TRACK	front,rear,ins.	48-80, 48-76	48-76, 48-76	52-76, 48-76	48-76	48-76, 48-76	48.52-76, 52-76	52¼-71¼, 52¼-71¼	48-70, 4-72
WHEELBASE	inches	72	73	73	74	76	75	73	76
LENGTH	over wheels, ins.	117	110½	118½	112	114½	113¾	111	115½
HEiGHT	bonnet line, ins.	54	47	54.4 to steering wheel	59½ (S/W)	60¾ (S/W)	51¾	55	57½
WIDTH	overall, ins.	64	64	64½	63¾	61	62¾	68	60½
GROUND CLEARANCE	inches	21 front axle	21 front axle	21 front axle	15½ transmission	16½ transmission	18½ front axle	16¾ front axle	26½ transmission
TYRES	front	4.00-19 (6.00-16)	4.00-19	5.50-16	4.00-19	5.50-16	5.00-15	5.50-16	6.00-16
	rear	10-28	10-28	11-28	10-28	10-28	10-28	10-28	11-28
BRAKES	type	Drum	Drum	Drum	Disc	Dlsc	Drum	Drum	Drum
	handbrake	Not available	Yes	Yes	Yes	Yes	Yes	Yes	No
ENGINE	model	A3.152 3 cyl.	F3 3 cyl.	New Super 3 cyl.	I.H.C. 4 cyl.	I.H.C. 4 cyl.	D.B. 4 cyl.	B.M.C. 3 cyl.	Standard 23C 4 cyl.
	horsepower	44.5 installed	32.0 bare	39.5 installed	35.0 bare	40.0 bare	35.0 bare	39.8 installed	37.0 installed
	torque lb/ft	119 at 1300rpm	92 at 1200rpm	112 at 1250rpm	102 at 1500rpm	115 at 1300rpm.	102 at 1400rpm	117 at 1400rpm	107 at 1500rpm
	governed speed	2250	2000	2000	1875	2000	2000	2000	2000
	capacity, cu in	152.7	144.0	152.0	144.0	154.0	154.0	155.6	138.0
	injection system	Indirect	Indirect	Indirect	Indirect	Indirect	Direct	Direct	Indirect
	governor	Mechanical	Mechanical	Mechanical	Pneumatic	Mechanical	Mechanical	Pneumatic	Mechanical
GEARS	number	6F-2R (12F-4R optional)	6F-2R	6F-2R	8F-2R	8F-2R	6F-2R	5F-1R	8F-2R
SPEEDS MPH	at max engine rpm	1.50-16.41	1.27-15.45	1.4-17.4	1.50-13.50	1.41-15.03	2.1-14.2	1.82-14.0	1.13-15.22
	min forward speed	1.12	1.16	1.26	1.47	1.42	1.15	.99	.93
DIFFERENTIAL LOCK	standard	Extra	Yes	Yes	Yes	Yes	Yes	Yes	Extra
PTO	engine rpm at 540	1700 (1500 single clutch)	1800	1800	1840	2000	1100 or 1800	1400	170
	1000 rpm	No	No	No	Yes	Yes	Yes	No	No
	ground speed	Yes	No	No	No	No	No	No	No
	horsepower at 540	35	28	34	31.5	37	31 (20 high ratio)	29.2	30.0
HYDRAULICS	layout	Integral	Integral	Integral	Integral	Integral	Integral	Integral	Integral
	draft control	Yes	Yes	Yes	No	Yes	Yes	Yes	No
	position control	Yes	Yes	Yes	No	Yes	No	No	No
	pump location	Transmission	Transmission	Transmission	Engine	Engine	Transmission	Transmission	Engine
LINKAGE	Comb. Cat. 1 & 2	Extra	No	No	Yes	Yes	Yes	Yes	Yes
	max lift, lbs	2500	1850	1850	2275	2600	1800	2300	2240
FILL-UP DATA	Fuel	8½ gallons	7 gallons	7 gallons	8½ gallons	10.6 gallons	8¾ gallons	14 gallons	16.8 gallons
	Engine	11½ pints	12¾ pints	12½ pints	9 pints	9 pints	17 pints	14 pints	12 pints
	Transmission	53 pints	53 pints	53 pints	38 pints	32 pints	31 pints	96 pints	16 pints